KINGDOM
DISCIPLES

KINGDOM DISCIPLES

Heaven's Representatives on Earth

TONY EVANS

MOODY PUBLISHERS

CHICAGO

Portions of this book are adapted from the following books by Tony Evans: *America* (Chicago: Moody, 2014), *The Kingdom Agenda* (Chicago: Moody, 2013), *Oneness Embraced* (Chicago: Moody, 2011), *The Transforming Word* (Chicago: Moody, 2006), *What Matters Most* (Chicago: Moody, 2002), *Free at Last* (Chicago: Moody, 2005), and *Life Essentials for Knowing God Better, Experiencing God Deeper, Loving God More* (Chicago: Moody, 2007).

Edited by Jim Vincent
Interior and Cover design: Erik M. Peterson
Cover image of crowd at station courtesy of Nicolai Berntsen/Unsplash.

ISBN: 978-0-8024-1203-4

We hope you enjoy this book from Moody Publishers. Our goal is to provide high-quality, thought-provoking books and products that connect truth to your real needs and challenges. For more information on other books and products written and produced from a biblical perspective, go to www.moodypublishers.com or write to:

Moody Publishers
820 N. LaSalle Boulevard
Chicago, IL 60610

1 3 5 7 9 10 8 6 4 2

Printed in the United States of America

*Gratefully dedicated to all the
kingdom agenda pastors we are privileged
to serve through The Urban Alternative.*

Contents

Introduction: The Need for Kingdom Disciples   9

Part 1: The Foundation of Kingdom Discipleship

1. The Missing Key   15
2. The Primary Concern   37
3. The Bold Confession   55
4. The Cost of Commitment   77

Part 2: The Formation of Kingdom Discipleship

5. Our True Identity   95
6. A Deep Intimacy   117
7. A Steady Increase   133
8. The Heavenly Incentive   147

Part 3: The Function of Kingdom Discipleship

9. The Individual   163
10. The Family   179
11. The Church   197
12. The Community   217

Conclusion   239
Appendix A: Kingdom Discipleship Action Steps   243
Appendix B: The Urban Alternative   245

The Need for Kingdom Disciples

When two teams compete in a professional sporting event, there is always an officiating crew to manage the game and uphold the rules. The teams in conflict, by the very nature of the battle, can never be expected to agree because they are headed toward two different goals. The officiating crew, however, has been positioned by the league office in the middle of the conflict but is not part of the conflict. Their job is to bring order to what would otherwise become a chaotic situation.

The league office gives each official a rule book by which all decisions are to be made on the field of play. Personal opinions and preferences are subordinate to what is written in the book. Even though the officials are outnumbered by players and the crowd and may be both booed and cheered based on the call they make, they understand that they are not there for a popularity contest but to rule on the field based on their delegated authority received from the league authorities they represent.

Likewise, God has placed His agents who represent His kingdom rule from heaven in the midst of the chaos on earth. His officiating crew is called disciples—people whose ultimate commitment is not to the competing races, classes, cultures, personalities, and political views of the culture but rather to His kingdom. These kingdom representatives have been given a book, the inerrant Word of God, by which all decisions are to be made.

The crisis we face today, however, is that many among God's officiating crew have joined the competing teams on the field rather than being the distinctly unique kingdom representatives He has left us here to be. As a result, not only is there confusion on the field of the culture but there is also the absence of the kingdom authority that should be being exercised by His appointed representatives.

It is the goal of kingdom disciples to advance God's kingdom agenda, which is the *visible manifestation of God's comprehensive rule over every area of life.* This agenda is carried out through His four divinely authorized spheres of the individual, family, church, and community.

The goal of *Kingdom Disciples* is to call believers and churches back to our primary divinely ordained responsibility to be disciples and disciplemakers. Only when we take seriously this assignment will the world see the supernatural power of heaven at work on earth and eternity operating in history. Only as God's officiating crew stops trying to placate the competing value systems of this world and begin making decisions solely based on the book we have been given from our King—the Bible—will we see the authority at work we have been delegated to exercise on His behalf.

It's time now for kingdom disciples to take the field and deliver heaven's answers to earth.

PART 1

The Foundation of Kingdom Discipleship

CHAPTER I

The Missing Key

One of the greatest tragedies of the twentieth century was the sinking of the *Titanic* in the chilly North Atlantic Ocean on April 15, 1912. Over 1,500 people died in the frigid waters of the Atlantic during the maiden voyage of this elegant ship that was believed to be unsinkable. The cause of the catastrophe is commonly understood to be the ship's hull being ripped open by a largely submerged iceberg, but the tragedy occurred primarily because of a lesser-known yet more strategic reason.

David Blair was the second in command, scheduled to make the journey from South Hampton, England, to America. However, on the day before the scheduled departure, Mr. Blair was reassigned. Mr. Blair had in his pocket the key to the crow's nest locker, which contained the high-powered binoculars that were used by the crewmember who watched from the elevated crow's nest for any potential dangers.

Because Mr. Blair inadvertently kept the key with him, the binoculars were unavailable at the moment they were needed most. Thus, the iceberg was not visible in the distance as it would have been had the binoculars been available. This ultimately led to the deadly crash we know today as the sinking of the *Titanic*.

If it wasn't for the missing key, the tragedy could have been averted.

Similarly, a key is missing in Christianity today. It is a critical key—its absence has resulted in weak, defeated believers, family disintegrations, ineffective churches, and a decaying culture. Without the full use of this key, followers of Christ lack the tools needed to fully live as heaven's representatives on earth.

What is the missing key?

You guessed it—it is discipleship.

Kingdom disciples are in such short supply that a bevy of powerless Christians attend powerless churches, resulting in a powerless presence and impact in the world. Until this key called discipleship is recovered and utilized, we will continue to fail in our calling to adequately live as heaven's representatives on earth. The power, authority, abundance, victory, and impact promised in God's Word to His own will be ours only when we understand and align ourselves with His definition of discipleship. Until then, we can anticipate that disappointments and losses will be the norm in spite of all the Christian activities we engage in.

Discipleship is the missing key to a life of authority under God. But surrender to Christ's lordship and obedience to His rule of love are the grooves that make up that key, which when used rightly will unlock the power to bring heaven to bear on earth.

A kingdom disciple can be defined as *a believer in Christ who takes part in the spiritual developmental process of progressively learning to live all of life in submission to Jesus Christ.* The goal of a kingdom disciple is to have a transformed life and to replicate God's kingdom values in the lives of others. Through His kingdom disciples, God exercises His rule from heaven to earth.

THE NEED FOR COMMITTED
FOLLOWERS OF CHRIST

After He rose from the dead, the Lord Jesus Christ took steps to ensure that there would be followers. He immediately called a meeting—but it was not any ordinary church committee meeting. It was held on a hillside in Galilee, not in a conference room.

This meeting was also different because of the people who were there. According to Matthew 28:16, Jesus' eleven remaining disciples showed up; it's likely another five hundred-plus witnesses also were present (1 Cor. 15:6).

But a third, much larger group of people was indirectly part of that post-resurrection meeting—all Christians, including you and me. At the end of the meeting Jesus said, "I am with you always, even to the end of the age" (Matt. 28:20). Since the age Jesus was speaking of hasn't ended yet, and since you and I are living in that age, we are also part of that historic occasion.

Let's read the "minutes" of Jesus' meeting:

The eleven disciples proceeded to Galilee, to the mountain which Jesus had designated. When they saw Him, they worshiped Him; but some were doubtful. And Jesus came up and spoke to them, saying, "All authority has been given to Me in heaven and on earth. Go therefore and make disciples of all the nations, baptizing them in the name of the Father and the Son and the Holy Spirit, teaching them to observe all that I commanded you; and lo, I am with you always, even to the end of the age." (Matt. 28:16–20)

No doubt you have never read any church committee minutes like those before. But even though this meeting included all the saints in church history from Pentecost to today, one of the problems preventing the current church from restoring the culture is this: we don't have enough committed followers of Jesus Christ. Kingdom disciples are in short supply.

Submitting to— or Resisting—Christ's Authority

Don't get me wrong. There was never any question about the ultimate outcome. God was never in danger of losing to Satan. But throughout history, Satan made every move possible to defeat God's plan and take over. He continually resisted God's authority and the authority of Jesus Christ, the Son of God. Satan even tried to make Jesus worship him. When that failed, he tried to kill Jesus.

Satan thought he had succeeded—for about three days. Hell must have had quite a party on the Friday evening of Jesus' crucifixion. It lasted all day Saturday too. But the resurrection was God's way of saying to Satan, "Sorry. You lose. My Son is alive, and all authority is in His hands. He's in charge."

That's what the word *authority* in Matthew 28:18 actually means. It means "being in charge." It's power resting in the right hands. When Jesus said that all authority was His in heaven and on earth, He was saying that He possesses the legal right to wield that power.

Now the idea of heaven and earth reminds us of the prayer Jesus taught His disciples to pray: "Your will be done, on earth as it is in heaven" (Matt. 6:10). So according to Jesus, a disciple's first concern should be that God's will is done on earth just as it is done in heaven. So how is God's will done in heaven? Completely and perfectly, no questions, no objections, no debate. In fact, Satan and the evil angels who followed him were the only ones to ever challenge God's will in heaven, and they were kicked out (Rev. 12:7–9; Luke 10:18).

So Jesus' plan is that there would be a group of people who function as His legal representatives to reflect and implement God's will on earth. This would be the role and responsibility of kingdom disciples. The discipleship process is designed to transfer Jesus' authority to—and through—His followers. That way, no matter where people live, if they want to know what is going on in heaven, all they have to do is check out the lives of believers individually and collectively. As disciples who submit to Jesus and to the Father, God's people are to exercise heaven's authority in history. Kingdom discipleship and authority go hand in hand (Luke 9:1–2; Acts 8:12–13; 1 Cor. 4:20) and involve the transfer of the rule of our King and His kingdom to the world over which He has been given authority. If visible authority is not being exercised then the full understanding of the purpose of discipleship is not being understood and experienced.

OUR ROLE: OCCUPY!

Since Jesus has already achieved victory and Satan is a defeated enemy, what is our role as followers of His who have been left behind here on earth? Jesus answered that Himself in Matthew 28, but He also gave a very succinct answer on one occasion when He and the disciples were nearing Jerusalem just before His crucifixion.

The disciples thought that Jesus was going to Jerusalem to set up His kingdom right then. Jesus, knowing what they were thinking, told them the parable of the nobleman who went on a long journey and left certain sums of money with his servants. Then the nobleman said something very interesting. He told them, "Occupy till I come" (Luke 19:13 KJV). In other words, "Do business for me while I'm gone. I'll be back" (cf. NASB).

I like that word "occupy." As Jesus' disciples, we're like the occupying army that a conquering general leaves behind in the conquered country to maintain stability and progress after the battle has been won. Even though Satan is a defeated enemy, he still has a lot of fight left in him, and he wants to take as many people down with him as he can. So our task as Jesus' occupying force is more involved than just sitting back and keeping an eye on things. The purpose of the church is to make disciples, not just add names to the roll or increase small-group Bible study attendance. It's not enough for the church just to be open a certain number of hours a week or offer a variety of programs. We are to make disciples.

Recall that Jesus gave His disciples—and the entire church—final instructions in Matthew 28:19–20, in what is commonly known as the Great Commission. In the original language, there is only one command: "make disciples." Three participles (action words ending in "ing") explain how to do that one command. They involve: (1) going, (2) baptizing, and (3) teaching.

WHAT IS A DISCIPLE?

But before any of that is done, it is important to be sure what a disciple is. *A disciple is a person who has decided that following Jesus Christ takes precedence over everything else.* Or to express it another way, a disciple looks and acts like the one he or she follows.

Jesus did not say being a disciple would be easy. Disciples have to take up their crosses and follow Him. In Mark 8:34–36, Jesus made one of the most profound statements in all of Scripture:

> If anyone wishes to come after Me, he must deny himself, and take up his cross, and follow Me. For whoever wishes to save his life shall lose it; but whoever loses his life for My sake and the gospel's will save it. For what does it profit a man to gain the whole world, and forfeit his soul?

The cross symbolizes an instrument of death. In order for someone's soul to become fully alive, it must first die to self. And it will need to die daily. The self-life, your selfish thoughts that dominate your mind and are in conflict with the will and Word of God, must die. Much more important is to save your soul, which remains forever, either in hell or heaven.

Yet in these verses, Jesus adds the teaching about saving and losing your life.

How do you save your life yet lose it? By going after the temptations of this world. When you do that you forfeit your life, because life consists of more than the stuff you accumulate. Many people have a house but no longer have a home. Many people have money but don't have peace. Many people have plans but don't have any purpose. This principle of saving and losing your life is fixed. It's another way of saying you can't find God's purpose for your life when you're busy trying to find your own.

Giving yourself totally to God is giving Him full power over your life as His follower. When you do that, you experience the abundant life He has promised you.

Years ago when the military draft was still in operation, young men were often called into the service at very inopportune times. It didn't matter if the draftee had just been married. It was good-bye bride, hello Uncle Sam. The same was true if the draftee had just begun a great job. As a new soldier, he now became the property of the US government. His new master dictated every detail of his life: when to get up or go to bed, what to eat—even how to dress, stand, and walk.

After boot camp, the military took a further step in controlling this soldier's life. It selected a new location for him, usually far from home, and a new occupation. If there was a war underway, this soldier might be sent to the front line where he might be killed, all in the line of duty.

If young men could be expected to sacrifice everything for their country, how much more should we as believers be willing to do whatever our Commander, Jesus Christ, asks of us? That's what is expected of us as His followers.

A Shortage of Disciples

Of course, not everyone who heard Jesus speak while He was on earth became His disciple. Whenever He drew a large crowd, He eliminated most of them by talking about the requirements of following Him. If Jesus were interested in just building a large fan base, He would have kept quiet about the cost of discipleship.

But Jesus wasn't playing the numbers game. He was making disciples. Unfortunately, most of the people who heard Him weren't interested in absolute commitment to His authority. Getting by and enjoying the benefits of Messiah was good enough for them.

Sadly, that's too often the case with Christians today. Too many of us serve Christ as long as He doesn't start messing with our comfort. We're willing to follow Him as long as He keeps money in our pockets and smiles on our faces. But we don't want to be inconvenienced.

"Yes, I love the Lord, but I'm not really interested in serving others."

"I want to serve God, but my job keeps me too busy."

"Wednesday prayer meeting is during my favorite television programs. But I'll give God two good hours on Sunday."

Few church members would ever say things like this out loud, but that's the message they convey. As a result, there are too few disciples around to enable the church to impact the world.

This helps explain why so many people go to church every Sunday in the city, yet the city doesn't change. It helps explain why countless numbers of Christians work in the cities of America every weekday, yet our country doesn't change.

The primary problem in our country is not that we don't have enough money, not that we can't work through the sociological problems, and not that there are not enough government programs. The problem with our country is not even that we don't have enough churches filled with Christians. The problem is we don't have enough disciples. Where are the true followers?

This shortage of disciples explains why we have so many Christians and so little impact within our own churches, let alone in the country at large. What we need now are not more bodies in the pews. What we desperately need are more disciples, visible and verbal unapologetic followers of Jesus Christ.

If we are going to see our country change, if we are going to see the suburbs, small towns, and rural America claimed for Christ, it will be because we make disciples in obedience to Christ's command and see them exercise the authority of heaven in history.

Until we become disciples ourselves and make disciples, we cannot hope to see change. The church in America will remain weak and ineffective, resulting in the continual deterioration of the culture. But there's still hope that the church can get its strength back if it moves from a focus on membership to a focus on discipleship.

READY TO UPSET THE WORLD?

Notice in Matthew 28:19 that Jesus told the people who were gathered at that meeting in Galilee to make disciples "of all the nations." So the concern of discipleship is not just for individuals but also for systems that affect people's lives, including government. That was a big job when the known world was the sprawling Roman Empire. In order for them to do that, those early disciples would have to be big dreamers and mighty doers. They would need to possess and carry out kingdom authority.

Disciples were not just sent out to build a church. Christ sent them to exercise dominion. That is why the Jewish leaders got angry when the apostles came on the scene (Acts 4). They couldn't keep these guys quiet. They jailed them and whipped them, but Peter and the others kept right on preaching Jesus. Later on, the Jews in Thessalonica said, "Uh-oh. Here come these men who have upset the whole world" (see Acts 17:6).

What was it that gave the apostles the boldness to stand in the temple and preach right under the noses of the religious leaders who had the authority to flog, imprison, and even execute them? What had happened to change their lives so radically?

The answer is back in Acts 2, in that upper room where Christ's followers were gathered together after His ascension into heaven. The answer came out of their own prolonged time for a collective solemn assembly. There were only 120 of them (Acts 1:15), but they were serious about Christ, about paying the price, about enduring the pain and inconvenience of being His kingdom disciples.

God knew it, so He sent the Holy Spirit to indwell them just as He had promised. Those men and women, dedicated to Christ and filled with the Spirit, started making disciples in exactly the way Jesus told them to do.

Although 120 isn't a large number, there is a big lesson for us in that small figure. How often do we judge the importance of a church by the size of its membership? When we do that, we're missing the point. It's not how many members are in a church that matters; what counts is the number of disciples.

I'm convinced that some huge churches in our country today couldn't find five true disciples. And in some small churches, many members are disciples. The size of the building means nothing about how well it produces true followers.

The difference between the church of the first century and the church today is that when those people showed up, people either got real nervous or angry, or they got saved. But either way, when those early disciples showed up, people got shook up.

Often when Paul came to town, a riot broke out. Soon after he became a believer, he had to leave Damascus hidden in a basket that friends lowered over the city wall late at night to keep his enemies from killing him (Acts 9:23–25). In Thessalonica, the enemies of Christ mistreated the man in whose house Paul was staying (Acts 17:5–9).

Paul was always starting something, but not because he was a troublemaker. Wherever Paul went, things started to happen because he preached Jesus. He lived and breathed Jesus and expected others to do the same.

Do you realize that Christ has commanded His disciples to impact their community? He doesn't want you to be just another resident of your neighborhood or church, or your church to be just another church on the corner, not making any impact for the kingdom. When Jesus was on earth, no one was neutral toward Him. People either loved and revered Him or hated and tried to kill Him, but nobody ignored Him.

The world is ignoring Christians and the church these days in a myriad of ways and on a myriad of issues because they are not witnessing the authority we speak about, sing about, pray about, and preach about. What's worse is that many Christians aren't interested in Jesus either; they've grown cold toward Him. What we need are people who are on fire for Jesus, people with a burning desire to serve Him, people so excited about Him that they shake up the church and the community.

You can't be like Jesus on your job, in your neighborhood—and, possibly, even within your church—and not have opposition. Tribulation is a part of the Christian experience, or it isn't the Christian experience. If you're having an easy time with it, if Satan never bothers you, you'd better check the direction you're walking. You may not be walking hand in hand with Jesus, and thus not reflecting Him.

READY TO BE SLAVES TO CHRIST?

The sermons I preach at our church are recorded on master compact discs. These masters are then put on a duplicating machine to produce CDs for our church members and to listeners of our national radio ministry, The Urban Alternative.

There is only one master CD for each message, but of course this master can produce any number of duplicates. It's interesting that the duplicating machine into which the blank CDs are placed to receive the master's message is called the "slave unit." The task of the slave unit is not to create its own message, or to distort the message it is receiving, but to faithfully record and play back what is said on the master.

That's a picture of the discipleship process. Jesus is the Master, and we are His slaves (Eph. 6:6) with the task of reflecting and replicating His character and conduct and rule in history. It would be through the mass producing of disciples on a local, national, and international scale that would fulfill God's original intent to rule through mankind.

Discipleship was not a new idea in New Testament times. It was a well-established concept in the Greek world in the centuries before Christ. The word disciple means "learner, student," and the Greeks had disciples in the realm of philosophy.

In Matthew 10:24–25, Jesus described what a disciple should look like. We read, "A disciple is not above his teacher, nor a slave above his master. It is enough for the disciple that he become as his teacher, and the slave as his master."

THE GOAL

The goal of discipleship is conformity to the Savior, being transformed into the image or likeness of Christ (Rom. 8:29; 2 Cor. 3:17–18) in our character, conduct, attitudes, and actions. Discipleship also results in the exercise of His authority through us in the world.

A pastor friend of mine was visiting a college campus several years ago. He didn't know that my son Anthony Jr. was a student there. He said he was walking across campus and saw a young man off in the distance.

My friend said he looked and then stopped dead in his tracks. "That has to be Tony Evans's son," he told himself. "He looks like Tony; he's built like Tony; he even walks like Tony."

He was right, of course. The young man he had spotted was Anthony. Even though the man was a long way away, Anthony's characteristics were so obviously like mine that my friend told me, "I didn't even know Anthony was in college yet. All I knew was that nobody could look that much like you and not be yours."

In the same way, people ought to be able to tell by the way you walk and talk, by the total orientation of your life, that you belong to Christ, because nobody could function the way you function and not know Him. They can only conclude, "That person has to be a follower of Jesus Christ."

The family resemblance ought to be obvious. That is discipleship. It means to so pattern your life after Christ, to follow Him so closely, that you speak, act, and think like Him and help others to do the same.

We have Jesus' authority and command to make disciples. This is exciting because it means that He is with us in the process to ensure that it works when we do it right.

JESUS' PLAN FOR MAKING DISCIPLES

Now that we know what a disciple is, let's take a closer look at Jesus' three-step plan in Matthew 28:19–20 for making disciples.

It may seem simple, but it requires commitment and trust in Jesus if we are to follow His plan for making disciples. The plan involves three elements: (1) going to people, (2) helping people identify with Christ, and (3) teaching people Christ's commands so they may obey and honor Him.

1. Go to People

The first of the three things we need to do to make disciples involves going. As mentioned earlier, the original Greek of Matthew 28:19 can be translated, "As you go, make disciples." In other words, Jesus expects us to be going out. We could even say that our going is assumed.

What we are talking about is the ministry of evangelism. You can't make disciples out of unrepentant sinners. They must repent and they can only do so when they hear, understand, and respond to the gospel. Notice that the nations are not told to come to Christians for the gospel. We need to go to the people of the nations. Christians are not doing the work of the church if we are not winning souls to Christ and bearing public witness to the message of the gospel.

We must keep evangelism front and center in the life of the church. If the church is to grow by making disciples, its people must be willing to go into the whole world as Christ's witnesses. That's one reason Jesus sent us the Holy Spirit. "You will receive power when the Holy Spirit has come upon you; and you shall be My witnesses . . . even to the remotest part of the earth" (Acts 1:8). The absence of evangelism is proof positive that the work of the Spirit is not occurring in the life of a believer or the church. You may call it fear, or lack of opportunity, but the Spirit whose fruit includes love and peace (Gal 5:22) will give you boldness and opportunity to speak on His behalf.

Evangelism can be defined as sharing the good news of Christ's substitutionary death and resurrection and His free offer of forgiveness for sin and eternal life to all who come to Him by faith to receive it. Evangelism is done with the clear intent of bringing the hearer to faith in Jesus Christ for salvation. People must be born from above into the kingdom before they can be developed into disciples of the kingdom. The church, then, must challenge, encourage, and equip its members to effectively share their faith with unbelievers.

2. Help People Identify with Christ

Jesus said that another part of making disciples is baptizing those to whom we have gone and who have accepted Christ. He was not telling us simply to get people wet. There is much more to baptism than just undergoing a ritual involving water. In fact, the primary meaning of the Greek word for baptism is "identification."

Baptism was a very picturesque word in New Testament days. It was used of dipping a cloth into a dye so that the cloth became completely identified with the dye by absorbing its color. The cloth was immersed in the dye until it took on the character of the dye. The cloth underwent a complete identity change.

This is the picture behind Romans 6:3–4, where Paul wrote,

> Do you not know that all of us who have been baptized into Christ Jesus have been baptized into His death? Therefore we have been buried with Him through baptism into death, so that as Christ was raised from the dead through the glory of the Father, so we too might walk in newness of life.

When we put our trust in Christ, we became so completely identified with Him that His death and resurrection to new life became our death and resurrection. When we immerse believers in the waters of baptism, we are picturing their death to the old life and resurrection to a new way of life. That happened the moment they trusted Christ, but the ordinance of water baptism was given to the church as an outward testimony to this inward change.

Many Christians struggle in their daily lives because they don't understand their new identity. They don't know who they are in Christ. We have to realize that being "in Christ" is such a radically new way of life that whatever happens to Christ happens to us. That's why the Bible says that when Christ died we died, and when Christ arose from the dead we arose.

It's like putting a letter in an envelope and sealing it shut. When I do that, I don't have to ask where the letter is because the letter is safely sealed inside the envelope. So wherever the envelope goes, the letter will go too—and it's against the law for anyone but the recipient of that sealed envelope to break that seal.

Believers are now citizens of a new kingdom (Col. 1:13) and their identity and point of reference is to be in line with that of their new King. They are to be Trinitarians (Father, Son, Holy Spirit), reflecting the rule of God in all that they do.

3. Teach People Biblical Truth

Once people have believed the gospel and have been identified with Christ, we must teach them "to observe all that I commanded you" (Matt. 28:20).

I'm a seminary graduate and a Bible teacher, so I can really get into this one. But teaching the nations involves more than teaching them theology, Christology, soteriology (spiritual salvation), and all the other "ologies" of the faith. Jesus said the goal is that people "observe," or obey, all that He commanded us. Unfortunately, many Christians want to audit the Christian life like a college student does a class. They want the information without incurring any course responsibility. The result is that they don't get credit for the course. Information must be combined with obedience in order for heavenly representation to be authorized. Thus accountability must be a key component of our instruction since obedience is the goal.

Of course, our teaching must have solid content, because Christians are people of the truth and people of the Book. Jesus' commands that we are to obey are contained in the Word. But the goal is not content alone. The church today has too many "spiritual bulimics" who take in the Word at church on Sunday, but then throw it up as soon as they get home so it doesn't do them any good.

The goal of biblical teaching is to combine information and knowledge with skill in applying the truth to daily life. If you are sick and need surgery, you don't just want a doctor with an academic medical degree. You also want one who has skillfully performed the surgery before. That's why, for example, after Jesus had taught the people and then fed four thousand (Mark 8:1–9), He "immediately" had His disciples get into a boat and head out (v. 10).

Why? According to Mark 8:14–21, one reason was that He wanted them to apply the lesson they had just learned about His power to meet their needs. There wasn't enough food on board for the group, and the disciples were trying to figure out what they were going to eat. So Jesus asked them some pointed questions that ended with, "Do you not yet understand?" (v. 21). Obviously they didn't, but you can be sure they thought about it for a long time and eventually the message got through.

Making disciples is a process of spiritual development. It's similar to film processing, in which you take your negatives to the developer, who turns them into positives with the result that your pictures look the way they are supposed to look. God wants to take the negatives in our lives into His darkroom and turn them into positives so that we come out looking like His Son. The church and its ministry provides that darkroom where believers are brought to spiritual maturity through accountable relationships.

COMMITTING TO THE KINGDOM

Unless you are committed to becoming a kingdom disciple, you will not experience kingdom authority. In fact, since Jesus' instructions to make disciples is an imperative, to not be involved in the discipleship process is to be in disobedience, which is sin. Jesus concludes His instruction with the promise that He will be with us always (Matt. 28:20). This is not primarily a general promise to all believers but rather a specific promise to disciples and disciplemakers. There is a direct correlation between the kingdom, discipleship, and the exercise of authority. The greater and deeper the discipleship, the greater the access to kingdom authority. The lower the degree of discipleship, the lower the experience of kingdom authority. Jesus does not share His rule with all believers equally, for He knows what is in our heart (John 2:23–25). If we are not trustworthy, our authority will be limited.

You may say, "Tony, I'm a Christian, but I don't have a sense that I am living as a kingdom disciple, exercising kingdom authority, and I'm also not making disciples out of others." Perhaps that's because you have not fully committed to the kingdom.

A man once became lost in the desert. His throat was parched, and he knew he wouldn't live much longer if he didn't get some water.

Just then off in the distance he saw a little old shack. He made his way to the shack and found a pump inside with a jug of water sitting next to it. He reached for the jug to take a drink only to find this note on the jug: "The pump will give you all the water you need. But in order to prime the pump, you must pour in all the water in the jug."

This man had a dilemma. Should he drink the water in the jug and then be out of water and perhaps be unable to get more, or should he believe the note and use the water he had to prime the pump?

He began to think through his choices. "Suppose I pour all my water in the pump and nothing happens? I not only lose the water; I may lose my life.

"On the other hand, if there is a well underneath this pump and I use the water I have to prime it, then I can get all the water I need."

This thirsty man's dilemma is the question we have to ask ourselves as Christians. Do we get all we can get now because there might not be much later, or do we give up what we can get now because of all that's available if we are willing to take the risk of committing ourselves to Christ?

The man thought for a moment and then decided to take the risk. He poured the contents of the jug into the pump and began to work the handle. Sweat broke out on his forehead as nothing happened at first.

But as he pumped, a few drops of water appeared, and then came a huge gush. He drank all he wanted, took a bath, then filled up every other container he could find in the shack.

Because he was willing to give up momentary satisfaction, the man got all the water he needed. Now the note also said, "After you have finished, please refill the jug for the next traveler." The man refilled the jug then added to the note, "Please prime the pump. Believe me, it works."

We need to prime the pump. Some of us are half-stepping on Christ. We're trying to live in two worlds at the same time. We want to be sacred and secular, worldly and spiritual. We want to love God and love this world order. But my charge to you to remember is this: you can have the world if you want it—you just can't have the world and God (1 John 2:15–17).

You have to pour all the water—give God everything you have—if you want God to pour His covenantal blessings back on you and share in His authority with you as His kingdom representative. Only in the domain of the kingdom will you discover God's abundance and power to experience personal victory in your life.

CHAPTER 2

The Primary Concern

Major department stores like Saks Fifth Avenue in New York have large display windows. In these windows "dummies" are impeccably attired based on the season and the fashions being focused on. The reason the owners of the department stores place the mannequins in their store windows is to advertise what their store has to offer the broader public, inviting them inside. These mannequins exist for something greater than themselves, to advertise something bigger than themselves.

Even so, God saved us and blessed us not merely for ourselves alone but to serve as God's advertising agency of His greater kingdom. As kingdom disciples, His people are to make His kingdom so attractive that observers not only admire them, but are drawn to the kingdom because of how impressive we look and live as its official representatives. This is why the primary concern of disciples of Jesus Christ must be the prioritization of God's kingdom.

Again, a kingdom disciple is a believer who takes part in the spiritual development process of progressively learning to live all of life under the lordship of Jesus Christ. To live all of life under Christ presumes that we know and apply what Christ desires us to do in our lives. That's why I've chosen to begin with focusing on the longest sermon Jesus preached while on earth, which is known to us as the Sermon on the Mount. This sermon takes up three full chapters of Matthew's gospel (5–7), and it is addressed to believers—originally to His disciples. Christ's Sermon on the Mount is primarily a sermon about the kingdom delivered to disciples. So where better a place to dig deep in our study on kingdom disciples than right at the heart of what Jesus had to say regarding it?

The Centerpiece of Kingdom Living: Matthew 6:33

For starters, the centerpiece of Jesus' sermon revolves around one verse. In fact, this one verse is the centerpiece of kingdom living altogether. We read, "But seek first His kingdom and His righteousness, and all these things will be added to you" (Matt. 6:33). Discipleship is first and foremost a kingdom issue. Kingdom means "rule" or "authority." To be a kingdom disciple is to learn to comprehensively submit yourself to the rule of God in every area of your life. It is the pursuit and prioritization of the kingdom that is the chief concern of discipleship.

The word that I want to focus on from this passage is "first," because it is the diminishing of the value of this word that has led to the diminishing of the experience of God in many of our lives. The rule, authority, and provisions of heaven can be fully experienced only when God's kingdom standards are made the top priority of His disciples.

To experience life to its fullest and to accomplish and experience all that God has created you to do, God and His kingdom must be first. The problem in most of our lives today is that God is merely in the vicinity; He is not first. I often hear people tell me that they just don't have enough time for God, which means that they are really telling me that God is not first place in their lives. This is because a person will always make time for what is first, for what matters most.

PUTTING FIRST THINGS FIRST

Over and over in Scripture we read about God asking that we offer Him the "first fruits" of all that He has given to us. As just one example of many, we read in Proverbs, "Honor the LORD from your wealth and from the first of all your produce" (3:9). When Jesus reproved the church at Ephesus, as recorded in the book of Revelation, He chided them for having left their "first love" (Rev. 2:4). Jesus wasn't saying that they didn't love Him. In fact, He applauded them for being upstanding people who had "perseverance and . . . endured for My name's sake, and [had] not grown weary" (v. 3). Yet they had left their "first love." They no longer regarded Him as first in their hearts or in their lives.

In Colossians, this point of Christ's preeminence over all things is further emphasized where we read, "He is also head of the body, the church; and He is the beginning, the firstborn from the dead, so that He Himself will come to have *first place* in everything" (Col. 1:18, emphasis added). God makes it clear repeatedly throughout Scripture that nothing less than first is where He belongs in our lives.

Most of us who own homes have what are called "living rooms." However, these rooms are misnamed. They should be called "visiting rooms" because the majority of us live in the den, kitchen, or the family room. I remember when I was growing up in Baltimore that if I stepped foot into the "living room," I was quickly told, in no uncertain terms, to get out of it immediately. In fact, even when I go back there to visit now, no one lives in that living room at all. It's barely used, and still has plastic covering the furniture. This is because the "living room" to many people is simply reserved for special times or special guests. It's the living room, even though few people ever live in. It is misnamed.

Many of us have misnamed God. We call Him "Lord God" but He is only good for the visiting room in our lives. We visit Him on Sunday and we visit Him in our devotional times, but we do not live with Him. We do not spend the majority of our time in His presence. What is missing for so many people is the principle of *first*. Jesus said that we are to "seek *first*" God and His kingdom, above all else in our lives. A kingdom disciple does nothing less than that.

When the God that you acknowledge is not treated as God, then you do not experience His kingdom and its benefits. Jesus says clearly that when you put God and His kingdom rule first, then "all these things" will be given to you (Matt. 6:33). Putting God first is more than a mere declaration. It is also the implementation in our lives of His authority (i.e., kingdom) and His divine standards (i.e., righteousness). Without this God is not first.

That doesn't mean that you won't have problems or issues in life. What it does mean is that you will be well equipped to overcome or get through those problems and issues.

What It Looks Like to Put God First

A key way to know if you are putting God first in your life is to ask yourself where you turn when you have a decision to make. When you have a problem to resolve, or you need guidance, do you turn to people first? Do you turn to your desires first? Or do you look to God, His Word, and His principles first? Getting God's perspective on a matter and then applying it to the particular situation you are dealing with is the primary revealer of God's position in your life and your position as a disciple.

If you are a parent, perhaps at some point you said these words to your children: "Why didn't you talk to me first? I just wish you would talk to me first." Often parents will let their children know that they could have avoided mistakes or problems in life if they would have simply sought and followed their advice as parents first. While this holds true in parenting, it holds even more true with God. So many people wonder why they are not hearing from God or experiencing His abiding presence and victory in their lives. God's answer to their question is simply, "Because you come to Me last. In fact, you go to the world—a system that leaves Me out—first. And then you only come to Me when none of that works out."

The key to success as a kingdom disciple is found in this monosyllabic word first. It is only by prioritizing the rule of God over every area of our lives that we find the power of kingdom living.

When Worries Disappear

The context in which we read Matthew 6:33 is critical to its understanding. When we look at the surrounding verses, we can see a recurring theme appearing. We read:

> "For this reason I say to you, do not be *worried* about your
>   life . . ." (v. 25)
> "And who of you by being *worried* . . ." (v. 27)

"And why are you *worried* . . . ?" (v.28)

"Do not *worry* then . . ." (v. 31)

"So do not *worry* . . ." (v. 34, all emphasis added)

Did you catch the theme? Yes, it's worry. Right in the middle of multiple verses addressing our human tendency to worry, God places the very solution to our worry. We will look at this concept more deeply and how to pursue it in the chapter on individual discipleship (chapter 7). For now, notice the key idea: God says that if you will seek His kingdom first and His righteous standards first, He will willingly grant you all of the things that often make themselves the focus of your worry.

Friend, you ought to put God's kingdom first if for no other reason than to reduce your personal anxiety and worry. Over 40 million adults in the United States suffer from a diagnosed form of anxiety, according to the Anxiety and Depression Association of America. Countless millions more no doubt suffer from worry or anxiety on less severe levels. Worry is a common issue plaguing people today. Whether it's worrying about jobs, safety, health, relationships, income, terrorism, the future, or anything else, worry eats away at many people's ability to enjoy the gift of life that God has given them.

In Matthew 6:33 we discover the one principle that affects everything—even the level of your worry. God tells us in this foundational principle for kingdom living that we actually don't have to worry at all. God Himself—seeking His kingdom and His righteous standards—is the very antidote to worry.

A man was rushing one day to catch his plane at the airport because he was late. Worried he might miss his flight, he started weaving in and out of everyone walking to their gates with moves that would make an NFL running back proud. Bumping into one man dressed in a flight uniform, he paused briefly to say he was sorry. The man asked him why he was rushing so quickly, and he told him that he was trying to catch his flight.

> *Knowing and believing what God promises will remove your anxiety and frustration.*

"Where are you going?" the man in the flight uniform asked.

"I'm going to Austin," he replied.

"Well, then, relax and stop worrying," the man said with a smile. "Because I'm the pilot and that plane won't go anywhere without me."

Immediately the man who had been running through the airport worried about missing his flight was able to slow down and rest. This is because he knew where the pilot was. Knowing where God is located—knowing and believing what He promises when you look to Him first—will remove your anxiety and frustration on all levels.

Of all of the problems that you face—whatever the category —of all of the issues that keep you in perpetual defeat, have you placed God first in that area? Have you looked to honor Him first in your heart, attitude, choices, and thoughts? Have you sought His wisdom and will for you on how you are to respond to that situation? If you haven't, then go ahead and worry. Because you will need to worry. But if you have, then rest—God's got it!

YESTERDAY, TODAY, AND TOMORROW

Matthew 6 closes with a verse that many have found easier to commit to heart rather than commit to practice. It says, "So do not worry about tomorrow; for tomorrow will care for itself. Each day has enough trouble of its own" (v. 34). Most people are being crucified between two thieves: yesterday and tomorrow. They feel tortured today because of what happened yesterday, and they are too scared today because of what may happen tomorrow. Do you know that today is the tomorrow you worried about yesterday? In other words, as long as you are on earth, you will never run out of tomorrows. There will always be a tomorrow. So until you learn to make today what today is supposed to be—to embrace today, to seize it—you will perpetually live your life either being bound by yesterday or tomorrow, or even chained between both.

I would like to challenge you to change one thing. Put God first, not second or third. When you do—as a fully committed kingdom disciple—all else will fall in place.

Make God first in your thoughts, hopes, and decisions.

Put Him first in how you spend your time.

Place Him first in how you view the world around you.

Please Him first, honor Him first, give to Him first—and everything else will get in line.

God doesn't say that to put Him first is a request. This is a demand from a deserving King. But when you choose to obey this principle in your life, you will reap the benefits of experiencing the abundant life that you may have in Christ. In other words, God's got your back when you put Him first.

A lot of people never get to see what it looks like when God has their back because they are out there trying to fix it, solve it, tweak it, and obtain it all by themselves. They never truly experience God overruling their issues simply because they don't put Him first. This is His kingdom and He is the rightful King—

putting Him anyplace other than first is foolishness.

Keep in mind, we are to seek His "kingdom" and "His righteousness." *Kingdom* simply means His authoritative rule along with the comprehensive visible manifestation of it in every area of life. *Righteousness* is the standard God requires for people to be rightly related to Him. It includes abiding by the governing guidelines He has set as the King.

In other words, if you are a kingdom disciple and you want to know the right way to go, think, act, perceive, react, or relate—that is called righteousness. Righteousness simply defined is God's standard for living. His kingdom and His righteousness are to be what each of us seeks first. Without them, we are wandering aimlessly around without the support and the backing of our King.

In baseball, if you miss first base it doesn't matter whatever else you do. If you have run past first base without touching the base, it means nothing that you touch second, third, or home plate. It doesn't matter that everyone in the stands is cheering you or congratulating you when you cross home. Because if you miss first base, then nothing after that even counts. The umpire will still call you out when the catcher tags you after you finish your run past home plate.

In living as a kingdom disciple, if you fail to seek God's kingdom first, all else is for naught, simply because He has established His rightful place of authority as first, and without it, you are on your own.

THE PRIORITY: SURRENDER AND COMMITMENT

When you look around at the Christian community today, you frequently see chaos. Marriages are falling apart; single men and women are struggling to be content. Debt rules. Addictions prevail. Many are faithfully in church, yet living in defeat. They conclude, "My Christianity is just not working." They are worn out, lonely, miserable, and frustrated, to say the least.

Many have come to conclude that either this thing called Christianity is not real, or it is simply not real for them. However, there is a reason why so many well-intentioned believers are falling short of God's best in their lives. This is because without the password called "priority," they cannot access all that God has in store for them. The way that you express priority is through surrender and commitment to God.

If you have a smartphone, it is likely that you have a password restriction on your smartphone so that if you inadvertently left it somewhere, a stranger—or even a friend—couldn't pick it up and read the personal information that is on your phone. Passwords are often critical to the whole process called access, and the password for victorious kingdom living is this word: *first.*

I've talked a lot about this concept of first in this chapter, but perhaps you are wondering, "Tony, what does that look like? How do I do this?" In one of my favorite chapters in Scripture, Paul gives us the visual illustration of what it means to put God first. We read,

> Therefore I urge you, brethren, by the mercies of God, to present your bodies a living and holy sacrifice, acceptable to God, which is your spiritual service of worship. And do not be conformed to this world, but be transformed by the renewing of your mind, so that you may prove what the will of God is, that which is good, acceptable and perfect. (Rom. 12:1–2)

The problem with many Christians is that they have trusted Jesus for their salvation, but they have not yet made a decision to become a disciple. They have not surrendered their lives in such a way so as to be a committed follower of Jesus Christ. The difference between a decision maker and a follower is simply *surrender*.

What Paul is telling us in this passage is that God wants us to present ourselves to Him. He wants us to put ourselves on the altar. You and I are to present our bodies—that means all of our life—to Him on His altar. Keep in mind, in the Old Testament times when a sacrifice was placed on an altar, the priest did not just put the head, or the arm, or a portion of the lamb on the altar. He put the entire being on the altar. What too many believers have done is put a portion of their time, talents, and treasures on God's altar and assumed it is enough. It is not. God wants all of you to be given to Him.

In fact, throughout Scripture we read that anytime God wanted to do something big for His people, He always required a sacrifice first. There had to be something present that demonstrated sincerity and commitment. Worship is not simply singing songs on a Sunday. True worship, as outlined in Romans 12, is giving yourself to God in your entirety. True worship includes surrender.

I like the story of the chicken and the pig. Both were walking down the street one day when they came to a grocery store with a sign in the window that read, "Bacon and Eggs Desperately Needed." The chicken looked at the pig and said, "I'll give them the eggs if you'll give them the bacon."

The pig stared back at the chicken and replied, "No way."

The chicken asked, "Why not?"

To which the pig stated, "Because for you it's a contribution, but for me it's my life."

Unfortunately, today we have too many Christians who are only willing to give God an egg here or there, and after they do so they think they've given enough. They wonder why God isn't showing up miraculously in their lives. The reason is because God has asked us as kingdom followers to climb up onto the altar and give Him our all. Sometimes believers will climb up on the altar—and then climb back off.

Our King has asked each of us to give our lives as a "living sacrifice." Quite literally, a "sacrifice" is a dead thing. So the truest interpretation of this term is that we are to be a "living dead thing." We are to be alive to God and His desires and will while simultaneously being dead to our sinful flesh and our own will. We are to surrender to Him. Surrendering is about more than simply yielding. It is about committing all your energy, emotion, thoughts, and actions toward Him. It is an attitude that shows up in everything and everywhere because God's kingdom rules over all. Therefore God deserves to be our first priority.

Surrender is about committing all your energy, emotion, thoughts, and actions toward Him.

This reminds me of the commitment of fans of professional football during the NFL season. Pro football is big where I live. The Dallas Cowboys can pack 80,000 fans into AT&T Stadium—105,000 including standing room for the big games. They gather to participate in a mammoth worship service. I call it a worship service because worship is simply paying homage to something. It means giving both honor and respect. And also attention.

Every pro football game has only sixty minutes of playing time. But this is an interesting one-hour "service" because there are only seventeen minutes of actual physical activity in this one-hour service. This is because the clock usually keeps running while the players are either in the huddle, breaking from the huddle, or waiting between the plays. The actual amount of time that action is happening on the field in every football game comes down to around seventeen minutes. Surprising, isn't it?

Yet that reality doesn't faze the thousands in the stadium and the millions tuned in via TV, radio, and smartphones. They don't care that seventeen minutes of play that makes up a one-hour game, or that the elapsed time including time-outs, halftime, and video reviews of close plays actually consumes three hours of their time. I know this because they continue to pay high prices for tickets and will remain in the stands if a game goes into overtime. Trust me, if my sermon ever went into overtime, the place would empty out. "The buffet is calling, Pastor."

Neither do the committed followers of football complain during the breaks that happen between quarters. Or about halftime. In good weather or bad—you don't hear anyone griping that they have to walk such a long way to get to the stadium. Instead, there is excitement on their faces and anticipation in the air.

Likewise, when the service is over some three hours later, there will be another hour or two hours to walk to the car, get out of the parking lot, and drive home. This seventeen-minute game has expanded into a roughly seven-hour experience when you count drive time, parking, and returning home. And still no complaining about that much commitment.

Once the game has ended, the followers of football seek more. On the way home they will turn on the sports radio to hear them talk about what they just saw. And once home, they —along with those already home who viewed the live broadcast—will watch game highlights. The next morning they will open the sports section to review what they had just seen.

To prepare for the next weekend game, those fans will listen to the same sports radio, or television networks, or read the same sports sections in the paper. They may even add some fantasy football in there. In other words, commitment to the football team of their choice will not seem like sacrifice.

Football teams are notoriously hit and miss. And yet giving them the respect and honor that exudes from an attitude and atmosphere of commitment doesn't seem like too much of a stretch for most people.

In contrast, God—who does not hit or miss but is faithful, consistent, a provider, and worthy of our worship—often receives attention only during grace before a meal.

We have a long way to go in our culture with regard to how much commitment we are willing to give the Lord as His disciples.

RELATIONSHIP OR RELIGION

What we need to be careful to ensure, though, as we seek to put God first in our commitment and priorities is that our actions are rooted in relationship rather than rules. Too frequently people will confuse structure for surrender. They cross off a to-do list and think that they have put God first. In actuality, if God is first you don't need a list because you will naturally seek Him, His heart and His way, in your own personal surrender out of love.

Whenever religious activity, however sincere, trumps relationship, the victory of Christ is no longer experienced in the believer's life. One of the greatest dangers in our churches today is for religion to replace an intimate relationship with the Savior. By religion, I am referencing the external adherence to exercises, codes, or practices in the name of God yet apart from God. Religion is anything you do for God that does not stem out of a heart connected to God.

One of the assignments that I had at seminary involved writing a research paper. I remember this particular paper because when I turned it in I was very proud of the work I had put into it. I had done my due diligence. I had controlled the material, analyzed all of the possible idiosyncratic elements of the various arguments. I felt great about my paper.

However, when I got my paper back from my professor, there was a big, fat red zero at the top, along with a smaller note at the bottom. In a hurried hand, my professor had scrawled, "Tony, great work. Great preparation. Wrong assignment."

It wasn't that I hadn't done great work, it was that I had done my great work on the wrong assignment. I had researched the wrong topic. As a result, I didn't get credit for what I had done. Living as a kingdom disciple is no different. It's not that there aren't a lot of people doing a lot of excellent things, such as helping the hurting, and encouraging the depressed. It's just that they've missed the priority of the kingdom. They've missed the relational connection that comes through voluntary surrender and intentional connection to God the Father and Son. They have not made God first in their hearts. And so they experience few victories and have little authority in their lives.

Friend, external observances—the rules of religion—can actually get in the way of a relationship. When you are motivated by relationship, surrender comes naturally. There is a story about a woman who was married to an ungrateful, controlling, and dominating man. She had been married to him for over twenty years. She did everything that was on his list, recognizing that if she did not she would be yelled at, shoved, and then neglected.

This forlorn woman kept a list in the top drawer of her bureau of everything that she knew her husband wanted from her. Every day, she would seek to cross off each item on the list. After two decades of her trying to please someone who could not be pleased, her husband died of a sudden heart attack.

> *When you are motivated by relationship, surrender comes naturally.*

A few years later, this woman met and fell in love with a kind, generous man. This man treated her with respect, honor, and dignity. She loved his personality, his heart, and everything about him. She had always considered herself to be a lazy woman because it would take so much effort every day to try and cross off her previous husband's list. She lacked the motivation to do it—and although she did do it, she assumed she must be lazy since she ultimately didn't want to be doing what she was doing.

But life with her new husband shed light on who she was. She had energy, focus, and diligence. In fact, in any given day she would do far more than what was ever on the list for her previous husband, and what's more, she would do it both willingly and gladly.

One day, while cleaning out her bureau, the woman found the old list. Noticing that everything on it used to be a chore and had now turned into a pleasure, she wondered what had changed. Then she realized the simple truth that relationship was a far greater motivation than rules could ever be.

The first man dominated through rules without relationship. The second man offered her a relationship that then motivated her response. The activity was the same—in fact, it was identical. But the motivation changed both the results and rewards of the activity.

Friend, God wants to be first in your life as your King, but He wants His relationship with you to be the motivating factor for you as His kingdom disciple. Otherwise, you are simply begrudgingly crossing off a list called religion and therefore failing to access the strength, peace, and power that comes by way of His love.

We serve a mighty God who is all-powerful, but never forget that He is closer than you think. He cares for you. His love is to be your driving passion in putting Him first. God doesn't want you serving Him only because you are supposed to; He wants you serving Him because you love Him. He wants your morality, prayer life, dedication for Him, and all else to be founded on your desire to cultivate relationship with Him rather than on religious duty.

Instead of being defined by what you do, He wants you to be defined by who you know and who you represent—Jesus Christ. This means that your race, class, culture, economic status, and political affiliation must all be secondary to your relationship with God. Let Him rule over every aspect of your life. Remember the one thing God can't do is be second.

CHAPTER 3

The Bold Confession

One of the ways that Lois and I made it through seminary on such a tight budget was through house-sitting. House-sitting was a coveted job of poor seminary students like ourselves because it gave us an opportunity to manage something far better than we had the ability to own at the time. When wealthy families in the North Dallas area would go away on vacation for an extended period, they would often call the seminary to ask for a married couple to come to live at their home in their absence. This way they had trustworthy people watching over their property while they were gone.

For a brief period of time, financially struggling seminary students got to live like kings and queens. These residences seemed like palaces compared to what students had become accustomed to. Also, when you house-sat, the owner would typically stock the refrigerator and the freezer full of choice food and then say, "Make yourself at home." In fact, the run of the property was generally made available with just a few restrictions.

I remember one particular occasion when we were house-sitting and the owner had a Porsche sitting in the garage. When he left, he told me that I could feel free to park my old, broken-down and battered Grand Prix and drive his Porsche instead. You better believe he didn't have to tell me twice. I drove that Porsche to school and back taking the extra-long scenic route. But my wife would always remind me when I got home, "That Porsche isn't yours, Tony." In fact, she would quickly remind me that the entire house wasn't mine. We were just managing what someone else had worked for and built over time.

God provided a house called Eden for Adam and Eve to oversee and manage. They didn't own it, but they were given the freedom to enjoy it, use it, and maximize it. In fact, they were given great freedom with only one restriction—not to eat of the tree in the middle of the garden.

Because Satan wanted to make himself the owner, he got Adam to intentionally rebel against God. Keep in mind, Scripture tells us that Eve was deceived but Adam went into his sin with his eyes wide open. Because of his rebellion against God, the crown that God had placed on him was removed. Adam turned over the rulership of earth to the devil.

Restoring Lost Authority

At the heart of the kingdom rests this concept of rulership and authority. God told the first Adam to, "Be fruitful and multiply, and fill the earth, and subdue it; and *rule* over the fish of the sea and over the birds of the sky and over every living thing that moves on the earth" (Gen. 1:28, emphasis added). God created mankind to rule.

However, man gave up his rule when he was tricked by Satan. The earthly kingdom that was supposed to be operating under the heavenly kingdom was transferred over to the devil's kingdom. Yet there was one problem: God had committed Himself to work only through mankind to bring about His kingdom rule in history (Ps. 8:3–6). He would not go against His plan. So in order to work through man, rather than independently of man, He had to institute another plan in history. He needed a second Adam. In 1 Corinthians 15 we read, "For since by a man came death, by a man also came the resurrection of the dead. For as in Adam all die, so also in Christ all will be made alive" (vv. 21–22).

Also, in verse 45, we read, "So also it is written, 'The first man, Adam, became a living soul.' The last Adam became a life-giving spirit." If you want to understand all of history, you need to understand one word: *Adam.* There is Adam number one and Adam number two, and through both of them is the simplified summation of history.

History is this process by which God is returning us to the garden. In fact, history itself will end in the same place that it began. The garden will be called the "New Jerusalem," the place being prepared for those of us who believe in Jesus Christ as Lord and Savior when we die. We often call it "heaven," but what many Christians do not grasp is that much of their time in the afterlife will be spent on earth. This is because God's purpose for humanity was earth. We will be living on a "new earth," with access to our transformed universe. And all of this is made possible through the reclaiming of rulership made by the second Adam, Jesus Christ. When the first Adam failed to properly fulfill the dominion covenant to rule, Jesus Christ came—as the second Adam—to reinstate it.

When the first Adam rebelled against God, the Bible tells us that death fell upon all of us (Rom. 5:12). Everyone who followed inherited the curse of death, from Adam to Moses and beyond (v. 14). His destiny was imputed to us as the destiny of the human race because each of us is "in" Adam. Yet God gave a prophecy in the book of Genesis that would end man's spiritual alienation. We read in Genesis 3 when God is talking about Satan: "And I will put enmity between you and the woman and between your seed and her seed; He shall bruise you on the head, and you shall bruise him on the heel" (v. 15). Bear in mind that "head" refers to headship—rulership and authority. The seed of the woman will crush the headship of the serpent, or the devil. In other words, God was saying that someone who would be born of a woman would overcome the devil and reclaim authority and headship over the earth.

THE SEED OF GOD'S PLAN

Most interesting in this verse is how God chose to phrase it. Normally when talking about a "seed," you would talk about the seed of a man. It is the male who carries the "seed" while the female carries the egg. God had determined to do a unique thing in producing a human being without the seed of a human man, but rather with the seed of a woman connected to His own divinity. Through this, He would create the perfect God-Man, Jesus Christ, who would then provide another plan, or opportunity, for regaining the rulership that had been lost by the first Adam.

His perfect plan reminds me of our own human plans, which sometimes work. In football, coaches try to have alternate plans. Years ago as the chaplain for the Dallas Cowboys, I would work out at times with the team, even running passing patterns with Tony Dorsett and Drew Pearson. Basically, I was fulfilling my boyhood dreams. Yet, at the same time, I was also learning some of their plays. One very simple play was called a "fly pattern": the receiver would "fly" down the field while the quarterback threw the ball long to try and score a touchdown in one play.

Often the team would add a "waggle" to the play. A waggle is where the halfback peels off to the side in case the quarterback gets in trouble. If the defense decides to blitz the quarterback and cut short his time to position himself for the pass, he goes to plan B, the waggle, and tosses the ball to the halfback. This alternate plan was sometimes available for the quarterback.

In a similar way the all-wise, all-knowing God had another plan for mankind. When Satan decided to blitz God's plan and attempt to "sack" humanity, God enacted His perfect plan. He tossed the ball to the second Adam, Jesus Christ, for Him to carry out the purposes of God in advancing His kingdom on earth. That's a play that Satan didn't count on.

When Satan first heard that God's grand plan involved the seed of a woman, he began a long quest to kill that seed. First he tempted Cain, who would kill his brother, Abel. But God then enabled Eve to give birth to another seed, Seth. After that, Satan sought to contaminate the seed of mankind when demon-possessed men had relationships with women (Gen. 6:1–4). Then, after mankind's wickedness increased greatly, God destroyed all of humanity except for the family of Noah (v. 5–8).

Essentially, you can read through the entire Old Testament, witnessing this back-and-forth scenario, as Satan wrestled with humankind, and men and women wrestled with sin and fell continually in the depravity of their sins, only on occasions coming back to God. After we reach the close of the Old Testament, we come to a four-hundred-year period of silence. Then the Bible writer Matthew begins the New Testament by giving us the genealogy of the seed of Jesus Christ (Matt. 1:1–16; see also Luke 3:23–38).

Until this time, God would use men to advance His kingdom on earth. Yet now God became a man in the person of Jesus Christ. Through a virgin birth He provided the opportunity for earth to become realigned properly again with Him and His kingdom. In Jesus Christ, both heaven and earth would soon become unified. Even then Satan once more would work behind the scenes trying to get rid of the prophetic seed, influencing Herod to issue a decree to kill every boy under the age of two at the time of Jesus' birth.

Because Satan's attempts failed, though, Jesus was able to live a sinless life, rise from the dead, ascend into heaven, and reclaim the kingdom that the first Adam had abandoned. Through the power of the cross and resurrection, today Jesus Christ has ultimate authority in our world. Satan no longer holds the final authority in believers' lives or on this earth.

POWER VERSUS AUTHORITY

God knows that and Satan knows that, but Satan doesn't want kingdom disciples of Jesus Christ to know that. So he tries to intimidate, pressure, and lie in an attempt to get kingdom followers to believe that he still has power over them. And the reason so many people are not living lives reflective of the kingdom of God is that they have lost sight of the reality that Jesus Christ has deactivated, dismantled, and disarmed Satan's headship at the cross.

God has given the ultimate authority over what happens in history to His Son. He has placed all things in subjection to Him. As we read in Ephesians, "He put all things in subjection under His feet, and gave Him as head over all things to the church, which is His body, the fullness of Him who fills all in all" (Eph. 1:22–23).

Yet often we don't live in light of this truth. The reason is we confuse the terms "power" and "authority." Satan still has power. He still dominates the world in which we live and influences people's lives in countless ways. He is as powerful now as he has ever been. His tactics and destruction are both real and damaging. But what he doesn't have is final authority. *Authority is the right to use the power that you possess.*

For example, on the football field the players are bigger and stronger—more powerful—than the referees. The referees are older, smaller, and more out of shape than the players. The players can knock them down—power. But the referees can put the players out of the game—authority. Satan has power, but the only way he is free to use that power over the lives of individuals, families, churches, or even the broader society is when Christians fail to operate from under the rightful headship of the Lord Jesus Christ. Satan does not have the authority to use his power when disciples function under the covering of Jesus Christ.

This is why Satan will try hard and long to lure people and divine institutions out from under the lordship of Jesus Christ. He knows that if he can get them out from under Christ's covering, he has free reign to deceive and harm them however he chooses. It is under the covering of the lordship of Christ that disciples stand protected. This protective covering in Scripture is known as a covenant. A covenant is the mechanism by which God oversees and operates His kingdom program.

Colossians 1:13 tells us that God has "rescued us from the domain of darkness, and transferred us to the kingdom of His beloved Son." God rescued us from the authority of darkness and out of the wrong kingdom. By rescuing us, He transferred us to live our lives under the rule of Christ. The word "Christ" or "Messiah" means "anointed one." Jesus Christ has been designated by the Father as King over the whole earth. The goal of history is to bring all things to recognize His rule (Eph. 1:10, 22, 23). Therefore, discipleship is a kingdom issue.

MEMBERS OF A NEW KINGDOM

Believers used to belong to Satan's kingdom and rulership before meeting Christ, but now Christians are part of a new kingdom of which Jesus Christ is the King. Satan, in order to rule the lives and institutions of kingdom disciples, must get them to leave the kingdom rule of Jesus Christ and come back over to his.

Much of this happens through the division of the secular and the sacred. People attend and participate in church under one kingdom. Then they go out into the world Monday through Saturday and function there under the influence of another kingdom. There are studies done of the Bible in one kingdom. Then there is socializing done with friends in another kingdom. Essentially, we witness this flip-flop of kingdoms and then wonder why there is not more victory and rule in lives, homes, churches, and communities.

The answer is simple: Satan is ruling the lives of Christians because they are yielding the power to him—not by way of any rightful authority that he has but simply because of a failure to align their thoughts and decisions under the lordship of Jesus Christ. Through abandoning the union we were created to have with Christ, under His headship as His disciples, authority is lost. By not giving Jesus Christ the proper place in our personal lives, homes, churches, and in our world—the first place that He deserves—we lose His covering.

All of life for a kingdom disciple ought to be summed up in the recognition of and submission to the lordship of Jesus Christ. After all, Jesus is

> the image of the invisible God, the firstborn of all creation. For by Him all things were created, both in the heavens and on earth, visible and invisible, whether thrones or dominions or rulers or authorities—all things have been created through Him and for Him. He is before all things, and in Him all things hold together. He is also head of the body, the church; and He is the beginning, the firstborn from the dead, so that He Himself will come to have first place in everything. (Col. 1:15–18)

With the resurrection and exaltation of Jesus Christ, He has been made the head over all rulers and authority. He is in charge. When a person accepts Jesus Christ as their sin-bearer, then they have transferred kingdoms. Jesus Christ is then to be preeminent in their life. He is to have first place in all things. Only as His heavenly representatives acknowledge and submit to the lordship of Christ can they make the power and authority of God's kingdom visible in history. God explicitly states that it is His intentional purpose to bring all of history under the rule of Jesus Christ (Eph. 1:9–10).

Transferring kingdoms can best be illustrated by what happens when a single woman gets married. When she marries, she is transferred from the kingdom of her father to the kingdom of her husband. She is no longer underneath her father's headship, but rather she is under her husband's headship. The surest way to have problems in a family is for a married woman to go to her father to overrule her husband in her life choices. When that happens, there is inevitably a conflict of kingdoms.

As children of God, we have been transferred from the kingdom of darkness into the kingdom of Jesus Christ. Problems arise when we start listening to the old head, Satan, who owns and runs the kingdom of darkness. This brings us in direct conflict with the kingdom of God.

Colossians 2 gives us an insightful look into the explosive and powerful nature of our union with Christ when we are aligned properly under His kingdom rule. We read,

> See to it that no one takes you captive through hollow and deceptive philosophy, which depends on human tradition and the elemental spiritual forces of this world rather than on Christ. For in Christ all the fullness of the Deity lives in bodily form, and in Christ you have been brought to fullness. *He is the head over every power and authority*. In him you were also circumcised with a circumcision not performed by human hands. Your whole self ruled by the flesh was put off when you were circumcised by Christ, having been buried with him in baptism, in which you were also raised with him through your faith in the working of God, who raised him from the dead.
> (2:8–12 NIV, emphasis added)

Likewise, we read in Ephesians, "Even when we were dead in our transgressions, [God] made us alive *together* with Christ (by grace you have been saved), and raised us up *with* Him, and seated us *with* Him in the heavenly places in Christ Jesus" (2:5–6, emphasis added).

To apply this truth to individual lives, if you are a believer in Jesus Christ, then when Christ died, you died with Him. When Christ arose, you arose with Him. When Christ was seated at the right hand of the Father, you were seated with Him. In other words, you were made to function in concert and cadence with Jesus Christ.

In order for you to legitimately access His sovereign authority over all things, you and your world must be aligned underneath His headship. This includes your thoughts, choices, words, and perspective. It is in properly aligning yourself under Him and His Word that His authority becomes manifest in your own life as you seek to advance God's kingdom on earth.

An individual can go to all the church services that they want, read all the spiritual books that they want—in fact, they can name and claim whatever they want—but until they place themselves under the comprehensive rule of God in every area of their life, they will not fully realize or maximize the rule and authority He has destined for them.

SEATED IN *HEAVEN* WITH CHRIST

God has appointed a regent—Jesus Christ—who has been elevated above all to rule over history. Believing in God is not enough to access the authority that comes through Christ. Calling on God's name is not enough either. It is the relationship with Jesus Christ that determines what happens in history because He has been placed above all rule and authority, and by virtue of who He is, demands first place. Because Jesus is seated at the right hand of God (the power side of God), His followers are seated there with Him (Eph. 2:6).

I know what you are saying: "But, Tony, how can someone

be in two places at one time?" Well, we do it all the time through technology. I can physically be in Dallas but I can also be on Skype in Chicago. I can be seated in my home in Dallas and participate in a board meeting in Atlanta. Through human technology, we can be in two places at one time.

Now, if man can produce technology that can put us in two places at one time, then don't you think that the Creator of the universe can do the same thing? You are physically on earth but you are supposed to be functioning from the position of heaven. You are seated with Christ in the heavenlies. What the enemy does is try to keep you physically on earth and operating physically on earth.

If he can keep believers thinking that we are here—bound by the rules of his kingdom rather than accessing the authority of Jesus Christ in the heavenlies—he can keep us perpetually defeated and keep our world broken. The only authority that is the final authority is that authority that comes from Christ. This means each of us must operate from a divine point of view rather than a human point of view.

Have you ever been watching cable television when the picture disappeared and the words "searching for signal" come on your screen? That's what has happened to many believers who do not live their lives under the lordship of Jesus Christ. They are cut off from accessing His rightful authority. It's not that they don't have the ability to access His authority, it's just that they have gotten an interruption in the signal. The enemy has been allowed to somehow interfere with the communication and alignment they have with Jesus Christ as His kingdom disciples.

OUR CONFESSION OF CHRIST

The word "confess" means to publicly affirm and declare where a person stands on an issue; it means to say the same thing. Part of alignment under the authority of Jesus Christ involves a willingness to publicly declare and demonstrate commitment to and an association with Him. To put it another way, if you are a secret-agent Christian, you have not made Jesus Lord in your life. We read in the book of Matthew:

> Therefore everyone who confesses Me before men, I will also confess him before My Father who is in heaven. But whoever denies Me before men, I will also deny him before My Father who is in heaven. (10:32–33)

Based on this verse, the question stands: if you were accused of being a Christian on your job, would there be enough evidence to convict you, or would you be found innocent of all charges? Jesus makes a clear tie between His followers' public acknowledgment and confession of Him before men and His confession of us before the Father. Now, keep in mind, Jesus doesn't say if you confess *My Father* before men then I will confess you before Him. It's easy to say you believe in God. People pour so many variant definitions into the one word "God," that when it comes down to it—just saying "God" doesn't mean a whole lot anymore. However, when you publicly confess Jesus Christ, everyone knows who you are talking about. The name Jesus is ultra-specific.

Confessing Jesus publicly can be compared to voters who publicly declare the candidate they are supporting. They represent their support in a myriad of ways, including bumper stickers, signs, and rallies. They are not ashamed of their connections. It can also be compared to a married person wearing a wedding ring. That wedding ring is there on the ring finger to make a public declaration that there is a legal and binding relationship with someone else. Now, you can be married and choose not to wear your ring so that no one will know that you are married, but I doubt your spouse will smile on that choice.

There are a lot of Christians today who have married into the family of God as the bride of Jesus Christ who don't want to wear His ring. Theirs is not the bold confession. They don't want other people to know that they are bound to Jesus in a covenantal relationship—the new covenant within people's hearts (Jer. 31:31–34; Matt. 26:27–28). Instead, like Peter, when it is not convenient for them to be associated with Jesus, they simply say, "I don't know the man." However, because of this choice, Jesus makes it clear that when they are calling on Him and He is acting as Mediator between them and God, the Father, He will also deny that He knows them. As long as a Christian is a secret-agent saint, then he or she won't be accessing or maximizing both the kingdom power and authority that is rightfully his or hers through the lordship of Jesus Christ.

Jesus declares that a person's willingness to confess Him becomes the marker of their seriousness about Him. It is much more than simply believing in God. In fact, Satan believes in God. Alignment under the lordship of Christ—putting Him in first place—involves publicly declaring and demonstrating an association with Him in both words and actions and by submitting to His rule over every area of your life.

When my son Jonathan played football, he was a fullback. The job of a fullback typically is to run interference for a halfback—only occasionally does he carry the ball. Instead, the halfback gets the ball and the fullback goes out in front of him to block an enemy trying to tackle the halfback. The fullback's mission is to get rid of the enemy so that the halfback can get through the line.

Jesus' full-time job as Lord and Savior is to run interference for each of us as His kingdom disciples. Satan, our enemy, is seeking to defeat us. He is seeking to overwhelm us. But what we need to keep in mind is that we have a blocker out in front.

However, Jesus has stated clearly that He's not going to block for any of us if we won't even acknowledge or confess Him. Why should He run interference for someone who is just going to deny that He is even there? I'm sure you don't like the feeling that comes when someone has used you. They have taken advantage of what you have to offer, whether in your home, in a relationship, at the church, or even at your work. They have reaped the benefits from you but they give you none of the rewards or even credit. It is as if you weren't even a part of the successes that they are now enjoying even though you were the integral part of it.

The next time this situation arises where you are called upon to help this person out, your motivation to do it well may be a lot less than it was before. This is simply because no one likes the feeling of being used. We are relational beings, and we appreciate being acknowledged in our relationships.

Jesus is no different. Why should He transform our lives and our world only to be forgotten? He is saying, "Confess Me before others, and I've got your back. Marginalize, sideline, or dismiss Me . . . and you've got your own back." The question for Christians today is: "Who do you want to have your back? You, or Jesus?"

CONFESS AND BELIEVE

In the book of Romans, Paul writes a great document on theology to the Christian church. But in Romans 10 he includes two verses that have confused a lot of people over the years. They read,

> If you *confess* with your mouth Jesus as Lord, and *believe* in your heart that God raised Him from the dead, you will be saved; for with the heart a person believes, resulting in righteousness, and with the mouth he confesses, resulting in salvation. (vv. 9–10, emphasis added)

In these two verses we read two things we must do to be saved: confess with our mouth and believe in our heart. The problem comes about because every other place in the New Testament that tells us how to get saved tells us that we only have to do one thing: believe (John 3:16, Acts 16:31, John 5:24, Rom. 4:4, 5). Yet in Romans 10:9–10, we have to do a second thing: confess. So either the Bible is contradicting itself, or this passage in Romans must mean something else.

The answer to that dilemma comes in the context of the passage. Paul is not instructing sinners on how to become saints in this passage. He is instructing saints on how to get delivered (saved). You must believe on the Lord Jesus Christ to go to heaven, but you must confess the Lord Jesus Christ to get heaven to come to you.

Let me explain. When a person accepts Jesus Christ as their personal Savior (i.e., believes Jesus is the Redeemer who brings one to God through His sacrifice on the cross), Christ's righteousness is immediately imputed to them as their righteousness. They are saved, in the eternal sense of the word. Yet when they make a public confession of Jesus Christ as their Lord, they receive His deliverance in the here and now, in history.

The word "saved" means to be rescued, or delivered. The reason a lot of people who are going to heaven are not seeing heaven join them in history is because they have believed but they have not confessed. In other words, they have declared within themselves whom they are trusting for their salvation. They have placed their faith in Jesus Christ for the forgiveness of their sins. But they have not made an ongoing public confession, or declaration, of Him as their Lord—through word and deed.

In biblical days in Rome, Christians would be brought before the magistrates because they were declaring Jesus as Lord in both speech and actions. The term "Lord" means supreme ruler or authority. The Roman authorities would attempt to get the Christians to declare Caesar as Lord, and deny Jesus as supreme ruler and authority. Believing in Jesus didn't get the Christians hanged or tossed to the lions for sport. Believing in Jesus as the rightful ruler and Lord did. There's a difference.

Frequently throughout the New Testament the disciples and the apostles regularly referred to themselves as slaves. Notice that the book of Romans opens up with these words: "Paul, a bond-servant of Jesus Christ . . ." (Rom. 1:1). A bond-servant is translated from the Greek word *doulos*, which literally means "slave." A slave is someone who has a master, or a lord. Declaring Jesus as your Savior takes you to heaven, but declaring Jesus as your Master, or Lord, brings heaven to you. It is in acknowledging your rightful place under Jesus as His *doulos*, or slave, that you get to share in his authority on earth.

The reason we may not be seeing more of God's rescue

> *Declaring Jesus as your Savior takes you to heaven; declaring Him as your Master brings heaven to you.*

and deliverance in individual lives, homes, churches, and our communities is because we have Jesus positioned as our Savior, but not as our Lord. We, the collective body of Christ, are not His slaves. We are not kingdom disciples. Keep in mind that the job of a slave is to do whatever the master says to do. It's as straightforward as that.

Unfortunately, today, Jesus has too many other masters in most of our lives with whom He has to compete. The important thing to remember is that Jesus is to not willing to be one among many. He is not willing to be part of an association, or club. Neither is He willing to be relegated as a personal assistant. Jesus as Lord means that Jesus is to be the supreme ruler and master. He calls the shots, and He is to be acknowledged in everything that is done. The problem is too many people want a Savior but don't want a Lord. Because of this, numbers of individuals today are experiencing the result of denying Christ publicly. They are likewise being denied by Christ before God, the Father.

How does this denial occur? Three passages in the Old and New Testaments give us insight:

> For whoever will call on the name of the Lord will be saved. (Rom. 10:13)

> Paul, called as an apostle of Jesus Christ by the will of God, and Sosthenes our brother, to the church of God which is at Corinth, to those who have been sanctified in Christ Jesus, saints by

calling, with all who in every place call on the name of our Lord
Jesus Christ, their Lord and ours. (1 Cor.1:1–2)

And it will come about that whoever calls on the name of the
Lord will be delivered. (Joel 2:32)

These are just a few passages, but we can see clearly from
them that those being addressed are already saved from an eternal standpoint. They are "saints by calling." The word "deliverance" doesn't mean salvation in view of eternity. In the context
of these passages, and the passage we read earlier in Romans 10,
deliverance is God's help in history. Calling on the name of the
Lord invokes heaven to join you down here.

Let me explain how this works. Let's say I were to call on
God to deliver me from something that I was struggling with,
or a circumstance that I was facing. It was entirely too much
for me to bear or overcome on my own and I needed to be delivered. So I call on the name of the Lord. When that happens,
God, the Father, turns to Christ, the Son, and says, "Son, Tony
Evans just called on Me because he wants to be rescued from a
particular situation. What do You say?"

Jesus' answer to that question will be influenced greatly by
the level of our confession. According to Romans 10:9–10, if
you have not also confessed the name of the Lord that you call
on, your request could be denied. To experience heaven's authority and power on earth, a person must be willing to confess
Jesus Christ as Lord, publicly, in what they say and do.

You believe on Him for eternal salvation. You confess Him
publicly for deliverance in history. Both His investment and
His involvement in your life hinges upon your public declaration through both words and actions that He is Lord. Paul told

Timothy boldly, "Therefore do not be ashamed of the testimony of our Lord" (2 Tim. 1:8).

If for no other practical reason than accessing the power of deliverance on earth, you must establish and declare Jesus Christ as Lord in your life and over your world as His kingdom disciple. You must open your mouth publicly and let others know through what you say and through what you do that He is your Lord and Master—that you are not ashamed to be associated with Him and serve Him. He is seated at the right hand of God in the heavenlies, as are you through His redemption on the cross. Access His power and authority through a public declaration of His lordship in your life. His blood has established the new covenant under which you are to align your life and world in order to receive its full covenantal covering and protection (1 Cor. 11:25).

You've probably heard someone say, "I plead the blood." What they are talking about is the blood of the covenant. You plead the blood of the covenant by being under the terms of the covenant—making Jesus Christ Lord of your life and ruler of your world is the heart of kingdom discipleship.

In Old Testament times, the Israelites couldn't just say, "I plead the blood." No, they had to put the blood on the doorposts in order to plead it (Ex. 12:3–7). It involved more than merely saying it. They had to align themselves within the protective confines of the walls and the bloodstained doors. Likewise, today, there must be covenantal alignment under the lordship of Jesus Christ in order to experience His kingdom power, authority, and provision.

When we do this, we honor His covenant in blood, the new covenant described in key verses in the book of Hebrews:

But now He has obtained a more excellent ministry, by as much as He is also the mediator of a *better covenant*, which has been enacted on better promises. (8:6, emphasis added)

For this reason He is the mediator of a new covenant, so that, since a death has taken place for the redemption of the transgressions that were committed under the first covenant, those who have been called may receive the promise of the eternal inheritance. (9:15)

And to Jesus, the mediator of a new covenant, and to the sprinkled blood, which speaks better than the blood of Abel. (12:24)

Jesus Christ is the Lord of the new covenant, the unique mediator between heaven and earth (1 Tim. 2:5). He is our Master.

THE KEY TO THE CHRISTIAN LIFE

I have a master key to the church. The key can open any lock. It's a master key. A staff person who works here at the church may have a key to their own office, and even a key to the section of the building that their office is in. But they are limited in which doors they can open.

Because I have a master key, I can go anywhere in the church that I want to go.

A lot of us are not getting everywhere we need to go because we don't have the master key. We've got keys for certain rooms. We come to church, hear a sermon, and receive a truth so we have a key for a certain room in our Christian lives. We must understand, however, that the key to the Christian life for kingdom disciples is, in fact, Jesus Christ as Lord and Master. The ability to live victoriously and advance God's kingdom agenda on earth comes through this unique master key called total surrender to the lordship of Christ.

Only as His people reflect the lordship of Jesus Christ individually and corporately as kingdom disciples will the world experience the rule and authority of God as the Creator intended it to be.

CHAPTER 4

The Cost of Commitment

How many times have you heard someone say, "If I had known what I was getting into, I never would have said yes"? Many times, probably. Probably you've said it yourself more than once. That's why it's important to know what it truly means to be a kingdom disciple before you jump in with a deep commitment.

Jesus calls disciples to follow Him even though there are no guarantees. In fact, there is often a cost associated with true discipleship. Yes, that's not a popular concept these days. But it's the truth since it's in the Bible.

In Luke 9 Jesus introduces us to three men from whom we learn great lessons on discipleship. Jesus didn't offer these men a special deal. What He was offering them was Himself, and that was all they needed. He didn't guarantee a roof over their heads. He didn't guarantee them a promotion at work, or even popularity in society. Being a kingdom disciple is not a sure way to success as the world defines it. Most of the early disciples died for their faith (John the apostle lived as a lonely exile on the island of Patmos).

Read that sentence again: *Most of the early disciples died for their faith.* Underline it and meditate on it. Don't bury it under the dusty annals of church history. Since Jesus is the same yesterday, today, and forever (Heb.13:8), His call to discipleship is no easier now than it was then. These fully committed kingdom disciples didn't die in a nursing home surrounded by family and friends. Most of the early disciples died brutal deaths, Peter even being crucified upside down.

Now, are you sure you want to be a kingdom disciple? This is not a fast-track ticket to the top. If you commit to truly being a kingdom disciple, there will be a cost. That part is guaranteed. Few are willing to pay those costs these days. That's why we have so few disciples. And that's why we have so little impact on the culture around us.

"Allow Me First"

Our biblical narrative takes place in Luke 9, as Jesus and His disciples head toward Jerusalem. A man approaches Christ and says, "I will follow You wherever You go."

Jesus replies, "The foxes have holes, and the birds of the air have nests, but the Son of Man has nowhere to lay His head" (vv. 57–58).

Seems like a strange answer to someone who asks to follow you, doesn't it? You can't place it in the category of "lead-nurturing" or being "seeker-sensitive." Jesus basically told the man that He had no permanent home and, if he chose to follow Him, neither would he. We are not told if the man decided to follow Jesus after that reply, but the context suggests he was not ready to be a kingdom disciple. He probably saw the hype, heard about the miracles, and wanted a cut of the action. He just didn't realize that cut came with a cost.

I suspect that the second man mentioned in Luke 9 was listening to Jesus' conversation with the first man. Jesus turned to this second man and said, "Follow Me" (v. 59). This is a different case right away, because this man did not offer to follow Jesus as the first man did. Most likely, he heard the first answer and had a greater context within which to reply. He answered, "Permit me first to go and bury my father."

But Jesus said, "Allow the dead to bury their own dead; but as for you, go and proclaim everywhere the kingdom of God" (v. 60).

When you first read this, it may seem a little odd, even cold-hearted, how Jesus talks about the man's father. After all, aren't children supposed to honor their parents? Yes, they are. That's why insight into Jewish culture sheds light on this passage that we may not glean on first glance. See, if the man's father were already dead, he would have been home. He wouldn't be in a position to ask Jesus this question at all. This is because the Jews buried their dead within twenty-four hours. So his question is only hypothetical.

This man stretched his semantics a bit to make his case sound dire. In doing so, he was telling Jesus that he wanted to put off being His disciple for an indefinite period of time, until his father was gone and all the estate and family inheritance was settled. Since he had just overheard Christ stating clearly that He had no place to lay His head, this man realized he'd better secure his own financial security first. Otherwise, this whole discipleship thing could wind up hurting him financially.

> *Kingdom discipleship always comes with a cost.*

But Jesus wanted nothing of that. He told him to be a disciple he needed to go now and proclaim everywhere the kingdom of God. Not later, but now. Jesus knew this man was asking for time to get his situation secure by waiting for his father to die in order to get his inheritance before he would go all in with God. When Jesus said "let the dead bury the dead," He was saying let the spiritually dead bury the physically dead.

Many Christians also do this. They aren't ready to fully commit. Maybe they are waiting for their careers to settle, the kids to be schooled, or any number of things. But Jesus made it plain that discipleship demands immediate obedience, or it isn't kingdom discipleship. Because kingdom discipleship always comes with a cost. That's what a cross is, after all (Matt. 16:24).

Now let's consider the third man in verse 61 of Luke 9. Like the first man, he takes the initiative. "I will follow You, Lord; but first permit me to say good-bye to those at home." That seems fair, right? You're getting ready to go away for a long time. You don't even know if you will return. So you want to go home, pack your suitcase, and say farewell to the people you know and love.

But Jesus said, "No one, after putting his hand to the plow and looking back, is fit for the kingdom of God" (v. 62). Wow, if Jesus were a preacher today, I wonder how many would attend His church? He sees through words straight to the heart and calls a spade a spade.

The man, however, wasn't just wanting to go home. He was looking back. In New Testament days, if you were going on a long journey, you just didn't shout a quick good-bye. The farewell party the man referenced could have lasted a long time. What Jesus is objecting to here is not a good-bye handshake. He's talking about family making a potential disciple look back and think twice about giving everything up to follow Him.

I can imagine this man's family saying to him, "You are going to do what? You are going to follow this man you barely know to places you've never been? You don't know how he is going to take care of you. He can't even promise you a hotel room! This is not a good idea."

But Jesus says anybody who looks back after starting out on the path of discipleship is not fit for His kingdom. Why is that? Because you can't plow looking over your shoulder. If you are going to plow a straight furrow, your eyes have to be focused forward. Jesus is saying that if we try to plow looking back, we are going to mess up His kingdom agenda. Elsewhere Jesus warned, "Remember Lot's wife" (Luke 17:32). She left Sodom, but Sodom had not left her. She heard behind her all that fire and brimstone raining down from heaven, and she began to remember her friends back there. She began to remember all her possessions back there. She began to regret leaving. So she looked back despite the angel's warning (Gen. 19:17), and God stopped her right there (v. 26). She was judged unfit to go any farther.

What a difference with Abraham in Genesis 22. God asked for and received Abraham's offer of sacrificing his son, Isaac. The good news is that when you give God your first and best, He gives you His first and best. If you make God and His kingdom a priority, He knows just where the rams in the thickets hang out.

You can trust Him—with everything. And in order to live as a kingdom disciple, you will have to do just that.

MAKING CHRIST NUMBER ONE

We can see this need to fully trust the Father—and the Son—in Luke 14:25–33, where Jesus spells out the cost of following Him:

> Large crowds were going along with Him; and He turned and said to them, "If anyone comes to Me, and does not hate his own father and mother and wife and children and brothers and sisters, yes, and even his own life, he cannot be My disciple." (vv. 25–26)

A lot of people cringe when they hear that. This text has been twisted and misinterpreted in all kinds of ways. Is Jesus overstating the case for discipleship?

Do we really have to hate those closest to us?

Wouldn't it have been less harsh if Jesus had just said, "Love Me more than anyone else"? But He didn't say that here, so we have to ask what He means by hating our family. The key to this is that Jesus is not talking about our affections. He's talking about our decisions. He is saying that when we come to a decision in life and your family disagrees with Christ's decision, your family will have to yield to Christ. Jesus trumps all. It's as simple as that. The issue on the floor here is authority. You and I must be willing to put Him ahead of even the most precious people in our lives if we really want to follow Christ. He will not be number two in anyone's heart.

Someone may say, "That's doesn't seem right." Well, suppose a man said to his wife, "If another woman comes into my life, you'll have to step aside and be second priority to me." Do you think his wife would accept that? I don't either!

She shouldn't have to, because she deserves to be the only woman in her husband's life. He made that decision when he married her. The nature of the marriage commitment means that everybody else is number two. No one should question you if you put your spouse first when making decisions that involve your time. Neither should anyone question you for putting God first, even ahead of your spouse.

There is to be nothing in my life that deserves my commitment and my passion more than my love for Jesus Christ. It is to be so high above my love for my wife and children that sometimes it may look like I hate them when I put His will, desires, and direction first. That is how it is supposed to be in order to live as a true kingdom disciple. If your husband, wife, parents, or children are dictating your decisions more than the rule of God, you are out of alignment. You are not a kingdom disciple.

You have put your hand to the plow and looked back, sideways, and every other direction rather than to the Lord.

God's kingdom must come first. His will must come first, or you are simply not a disciple. The Bible tells us to love our spouses and our children. But Christ is talking about what happens when it comes down to the issue of authority, priorities, and decisions. Is Christ number one? If you have to make a choice between obeying Christ's commands and anyone or anything else, you choose Him every time.

If you want to follow Jesus as His disciple, He demands priority over the closest human relationship you have. Adam learned the hard way when he put his compassion for or intimidation by Eve in the garden ahead of God's rule (Genesis 3). And humanity has never been the same since.

Discipleship demands a willingness to put God's rule first. Yes, sometimes that even leads to suffering for righteousness, which is vastly different than suffering due to sin and its effects. Jesus said, "Whoever does not carry his own cross and come after Me cannot be My disciple" (Luke 14:27).

WHAT IT MEANS TO CARRY THE CROSS

Crucifixion was a favorite method of execution for the Romans. They would tie the condemned man's arms to the heavy horizontal bar of his cross and make him carry it through town to the place of crucifixion. Jesus had to carry His cross through the streets of Jerusalem to Calvary. The Romans made the criminal carry his cross publicly to put him on display, to say Rome was right and this man was wrong. The convicted man's cross was his indictment, saying to the people who lined the path that this man was worthy of death because the Roman government had found him guilty.

Jesus is saying to us, "I want you to carry your cross through town." He wants us to so identify with Him that when we are accused of being a Christian, we say, "I'm guilty." When we're accused of loving and following the Lord Jesus Christ, we acknowledge the charge. "You're right. I'm one of His!"

That's one of the things it means to take up your cross, to be a kingdom disciple of Jesus Christ. It means to be on public display, to be identified with Jesus Christ in every area of your life. It means that if your family and friends don't want to be identified with you anymore, it's all right. You will still identify with Christ. It means that if your standards cause people to walk the other way, that's all right.

Jesus says to you, "Follow Me."

There's one other thing you need to know about the cross. When a man carried his cross through town, it was a one-way journey. He was going to die. No matter how much he wanted to turn around and go the other way, he couldn't. He was on his way to the place of execution. Earlier, Jesus had said, "If anyone wishes to come after Me, he must deny himself, and take up his cross daily, and follow Me" (Luke 9:23). Jesus was not talking about physical death, since you can't die physically every day. He was talking about a day-by-day orientation to life. This is the call to discipleship, not eternal salvation. It brings fullness, usefulness, satisfaction, and victory. This is what the Lord means when He says that those who follow Him will save their souls, i.e., life (Matt. 16:24–26; Luke 9:24–26).

Denying yourself doesn't mean just giving up something you want. It means saying no to your desires and plans for your life when they conflict with God's perfect will (Rom. 12: 2). It means placing God's kingdom rule over every area of your life. It involves funneling all of your decisions through His grid. There is absolutely no division between the sacred and the secular for a believer. Everything is sacred because God bought your life with a price. He governs every single word, choice, entertainment option, songs you listen to, your time, talents, and treasures. All of it.

Now you know why there are so many Christians but so few kingdom disciples. It's not a club you sign up for or a small group you attend. Being a disciple is a full-on, no-holds-barred commitment of everything that makes you who you are.

GIVING UP YOUR CLAIMS

Living as a kingdom disciple who visibly and verbally represents Christ requires that you relinquish all claims on every aspect of your life. Jesus gives us two illustrations of what this means in Luke 14:28–32. The first is that of a builder who has to calculate the cost of his project (vv. 28–30). No builder wants to put down the foundation of his building and then discover he underestimated his costs so badly that he has to stop building.

Jesus is saying that being His disciple involves some planning, some calculations on our part. You must plan to follow Jesus.

I could preach on discipleship at my church, and someone could say, "Amen, Pastor. I'm with you. I'm excited about being a disciple." Jesus says, "Just a minute. Pull out your spiritual calculator. Add up the cost. Make sure you have the spiritual capital it takes to finish, not just start. Evaluate whether there is anything in your life hindering you from being My disciple."

The Lord's second illustration is of a king who is on his way to fight another king (vv. 31–32). If this king has ten thousand soldiers and the other king has twenty thousand, the first king is smart to pause and consider whether this battle is a good idea. If he decides he's going to get wiped out, he sends a peace delegation. He says, "Let's make a deal."

The point is that there is no neutrality. The king either has to fight or make a deal. He can't just sit staring into space, or his army is going to be obliterated. If you are a disciple of Christ, Satan is coming after you, period. Satan is going to throw his army against you no matter what you do, because we are in a war. Since that's true, you'd better count the cost if you truly want to be all in as a disciple.

Weighing the Cost and the Rewards

In verses 33–35, Jesus brings home the cost of being His disciple. He can't really use people who aren't willing to love Him supremely, who aren't ready to carry their cross daily, who have counted the cost and said no thanks, who aren't willing to give up all they have for Him (v. 33). People like this are "saltless salt." They are useless to the kingdom and do not have access to its authority.

Once you decide to follow Christ no matter what, you will discover the other side of discipleship, which is the reward of being Jesus' disciple. Now, there really is no reward without the commitment of being a disciple, so focus there first. Before you begin adding up the rewards, you recognize and accept the cost. Jesus doesn't want you to start with Him and then give up midway through and turn back.

Love: The Mark of a Kingdom Disciple

In the upper room on the night before His crucifixion, Jesus spoke these very familiar words: "A new commandment I give to you, that you love one another, even as I have loved you, that you also love one another. By this all men will know that you are My disciples, if you have love for one another" (John 13:34–35).

Three times in this passage Jesus told His disciples they are to love each other. Three times He emphasized this key identifying factor of a disciple. He said that if we, as modern-day disciples, love one another, all men will know that we are reflecting Him as His disciples. So the question we need to answer today is, "What is love, and how do we do it?"

The biblical definition of the Greek word for love, *agape,* is *compassionately and righteously pursuing the well-being of another.* It is placing someone else's needs and advancement higher than they may even set them for themselves, and certainly higher than you set your own. It doesn't have anything to do with liking someone. In fact, you can love people you don't even like because love is an intentional choice to do good for another. Love is an action and a commitment. It includes a desire for the other person to be better off simply because you are in their life—and bringing the will of God to bear in their life.

Jesus distinguishes love from an emotional feeling, when He issues His statement on love as an actual command. "A new commandment I give you . . ." Jesus specifically uses the word "commandment" in relationship to love. We can rarely command our feelings to do anything at all. But we can always command our actions through the power of our mind and our will.

Jesus established a permanent relationship between being His disciple and love.

Love is the mark, the identifying badge, of a disciple.

If you choose to use your words or actions to belittle someone else—even if you do not agree with that person—you are not speaking or acting as a kingdom disciple.

If you choose to use your social media platform to put down another person, or group of people who do not view life the same way you do—you are not behaving as a kingdom disciple.

If you withhold affection, warmth, and affirmation from your family members (even when you are not getting along), you are not living as a kingdom disciple.

When your boss does not receive your respect and full effort at work, you are not working as a kingdom disciple.

Should your prayers fully focus only on you, your wants and your needs, you are not praying as a kingdom disciple.

If church is a place for you to get filled up, blessed, and inspired and yet you are not willing to help others at the church with your time or talents, you are not attending as a kingdom disciple.

As a woman, if your clothing choices leave little to the imagination for the men around you, causing a stumbling block and temptation wherever you go, you are not dressing as a kingdom disciple.

As a man, if your interaction with women seeks to manipulate or dominate them through smooth talking, compliments, or inappropriate emotional intimacy, you are not behaving as a kingdom disciple.

I could go on, but I think you get the picture. Love is the mark of a kingdom disciple. Ongoing love is one thing that is sorely lacking in the church today. Yet when you or I fulfill the command of love, we (by nature of the command itself) fulfill all others in Scripture. When we break the command of love, we also hurt others (Rom. 13:8–10).

> *When you fulfill the command of love, you fulfill all other commands in Scripture.*

Do you want to be a kingdom disciple? Then you must live, work, speak, and order yourself under the rule of love. Biblical love means I will do the will of God for you, whether you deserve it or not and whether I feel like it or not. It is this mark of love that magnifies and represents Christ to the fullest.

Do you know why so many believers are in pain over their

relationships? Because they have adopted the world's way of responding. Rather than acting on the command and will of God, they act out of their own will. Love becomes conditional. It is a tool used in the give-and-take of life.

Remember, Jesus loved, even unto death. For those who did not deserve it. Of course, a love like that cannot come from within our own sinful selves. It is provided through a supernatural infusion of the Holy Spirit. "The love of God has been poured out within our hearts through the Holy Spirit who was given to us" (Rom. 5:5). That is why it is so critical to abide in Christ and the presence of His Spirit on a regular basis. Biblical love can only come from a person who is close to God.

Years after Jesus returned to heaven, the apostle John wrote,

> By this we know that we have come to know [God], if we keep His commandments. The one who says, "I have come to know Him," and does not keep His commandments, is a liar, and the truth is not in him. . . . The one who says he is in the Light and yet hates his brother is in the darkness until now. The one who loves his brother abides in the Light and there is no cause for stumbling in him. But the one who hates his brother is in the darkness and walks in the darkness, and does not know where he is going because the darkness has blinded his eyes. (1 John 2:3–4, 9–11)

RECALLING THE LOVE OF JESUS

A kingdom disciple who abides in the light imitates Christ's love through his or her own life. Christ is our model on how we are to live as His disciples. Embedded in John 13:34 is the key phrase, "even as I have loved you." What does Jesus' love look like? It would take another book to describe this fully, but let's look at a few characteristics.

For one, Jesus' love takes the initiative. John writes, "We love, because He first loved us" (1 John 4:19). God didn't wait until we were lovely to love us. He didn't wait to be asked. He loved first.

We often put conditions on our love. "Well, when you start doing your part, I'll start doing mine." "You go first." But when we imitate Christ's love, we say, "Even if you never respond, I still love you." "Even if you never change, this is what God would have me do for you." "Even if you never repay me, this is how God wants me to love you."

Imitating Christ's love also means *meeting the needs God confronts us with*. Again, John explains what this involves: "Whoever has the world's goods, and beholds his brother in need and closes his heart against him, how does the love of God abide in him? Little children, let us not love with word or with tongue, but in deed and truth" (1 John 3:17–18).

If we love as Jesus loves, we will not ignore a need God has given us the ability to meet. The reason for having "the world's goods" is to meet needs. It's not just to have the world's goods. Far too many of us have gotten caught up in one of our culture's darkest and deepest blind spots—that of materialism and personal gain. The Scriptures urge us "to be generous and ready to share" (1 Tim. 6:18; see also 2 Cor. 9:6–11; Gal. 6:10). Kingdom disciples willingly give to others and do not consider the things of this world their own.

Imitating Jesus' love also means displaying a love for fellow Christians. Our love for one another will identify us to the world (and to each other) as Jesus' disciples. Because of love, we will have a powerful public witness (John 13:35). And our love is supposed to be public; it is supposed to be visible.

Remember, the love we're talking about is not just natural human love. Only the Holy Spirit can produce Christlike love in us. It can't happen otherwise.

Non-Christians ought to look at kingdom disciples and ask, "How can you love like that?" The question ought to be raised. Unfortunately, it rarely is.

Yes, such love will cost you. It costs you in the areas of deference, surrender, and service. Love ultimately requires laying down your will for the will of God, which is that you and I demonstrate His love to others.

The cost of being a kingdom disciple is often naively assumed to be something like moving to Africa or some other foreign land as a missionary. And while that is a cost, it is not the only cost Christ speaks of. He tells of taking up your cross to follow Him (Luke 9:23). The cross represents all that consists of our life—our rights, time, emotions, and energy—and offering them in His service for the betterment of another. Often, it is more difficult to do that at home than abroad—in the workplace than on the mission field, in the church than in the community at large—or even in our words than in our worship.

Love came in the shape of a cross. To do less than taking up His cross is to forfeit your duty as a disciple and fail to properly function as the kingdom representatives He has redeemed us to be.

PART 2

The Formation of Kingdom Discipleship

CHAPTER 5

Our True Identity

A person's identity is a critical commodity, especially in to-day's information-driven society. Your identity has great commercial value not only to you, but to someone else who might try to steal it and use your name and credit line to run up a stack of bills you can be left to pay.

Some people change their own identity in an attempt to make themselves acceptable to a certain group. These people may buy designer clothes or a certain kind of car in order to appear affluent. In the Western world, a major portion of commerce is geared toward helping people look, feel, and act as something other than what they really are because someone has convinced them there is something wrong with their true identity.

Confusing what we do with our real identity is an easy mistake to make, but the confusion can be deadly if we want to grow and thrive as a kingdom disciple.

Our Identity Begins at the Cross

The moment you placed your faith in Christ alone for salvation, God implanted a new nature deep within your being. This new nature, also called the new birth, is the reference point for your true identity. The truth of this is expressed clearly in Galatians 2:20, which has been my life verse for many years. This verse contains all that we really need to know about our identity as believers, condensed into one power-packed morsel. If you can absorb and apply what the Bible teaches in Galatians 2:20, you are well on your way to growing as a disciple because your identity is the key to your spiritual development. Here's the verse, written by the apostle Paul to the early church of Galatia:

> I have been crucified with Christ; and it is no longer I who live, but Christ lives in me; and the life which I now live in the flesh I live by faith in the Son of God, who loved me and gave Himself up for me.

The first phrase alone is jarring enough to let us know that something radical is going on here. "I have been crucified with Christ." You and I can put our names in there, because this is a done deal. We have talked about "taking up" our cross under the lordship of Jesus Christ, but that is not in reference to our identity. In this chapter, I want to look at how "being crucified with Christ" actually forms the basis of our identity.

Now, to be crucified is to die. We know that Jesus died on the cross, but through His resurrection and our coming to trust in His sacrifice as our Savior, He gives us life everlasting. And on earth, the Holy Spirit takes up residence in our life and helps us overcome the old way of life we inherited from Adam.

As Paul wrote, "How shall we who died to sin still live in it?" (Rom. 6:2). Our old self is dead and gone, crucified with Christ on the cross and buried with Him when He was buried in the tomb (see Rom. 6:4). Because that's true, we had better be looking for our identity somewhere else, since dead people don't exist. A key step in kingdom discipleship and our identity with Christ is recognizing our death to sin and the old life. This spiritual death means that sin no longer is the core definition of who we are. Sin need not rule our life. Our problem with sin is now a problem of the flesh, which is the house we live in, not the essence of who we are in Christ.

You see, too many believers aren't growing because they don't know that their old life, what the Bible calls the "old self" (Col. 3:9), is dead in Christ.

Paul wrote, "If we have become united with Him in the likeness of His death, certainly we shall also be in the likeness of His resurrection, knowing this, that our old self was crucified with Him, in order that our body of sin might be done away with" (Rom. 6:5–6). We have been crucified with Christ, Paul said. But many Christians would have to say if they were honest, "I didn't know that."

A union with Christ occurred at the cross that is often not understood, and because it's not understood, people are oblivious to its life-changing implications.

OUR DEATH IS SPIRITUAL

Even though Jesus' death on the cross was physical, the death we died in union with Him is spiritual. But that doesn't make our death any less real. You may be saying, "But I didn't feel like I died when I got saved." It's true that the impact or the emotions surrounding a spiritual death may not be as vivid as we experience when someone dies physically. You may not have felt your spiritual crucifixion when Christ came into your life, but, according to 2 Corinthians 5:17, you become a new person and the things associated with your old life pass away. Kingdom disciples are truly dead men walking.

So how do you make this real in your life? Romans 6:11 says, "Consider yourselves to be dead to sin, but alive to God in Christ Jesus." "Consider" is an accounting term, like "calculate." It means to add up the figures and arrive at the answer. God says we died with Christ, and just as Jesus arose to new life, as followers of the Savior we have been resurrected with Him to begin a new way of life.

God gave us a means of demonstrating this death and resurrection through the ordinance of baptism. As Paul wrote, "Do you not know that all of us who have been baptized into Christ Jesus have been baptized into His death? Therefore we have been buried with Him through baptism into death, so that as Christ was raised from the dead through the glory of the Father, so we too might walk in newness of life" (vv. 3–4). Baptism is not salvation, but it is a public picture of what Jesus did for us. Similar to the relationship of a wedding ring to a marriage, it is a picture of a bigger reality. As I mentioned earlier, when we go under the waters of baptism, we are picturing our identification with Christ in His death, and

> *As followers of the Savior we have been resurrected with Him to begin a new way of life.*

when we come up out of the water, we declare our identification with Christ in His resurrection.

We often hear Christians say, "Well, I'm just a sinner saved by grace." No, that statement devalues the radically new nature of what God has done for us and helps confuse our identity. A Christian should not say, for example, "I am a liar," or "I am an alcoholic," but "I am a new person in Jesus Christ who is struggling with the sin of lying or drinking." If you *define who you are by what you do*, you're starting with the problem instead of the perspective that you are a blood-bought, totally purchased, absolutely forgiven child of the living God who has a problem in some area. So *define youself by who you are*. Knowing who you are in Christ completely changes your reference point.

Are you beginning to see how this applies to living as a kingdom disciple? Let me give you two more facets of the Christian's new life that blow me away every time I read them. Paul said, "We have the mind of Christ" (1 Cor. 2:16). Did you get that? We now have the capacity to think God's thoughts after Him. This new mind also includes our emotions, desires, attitudes, and all of the other components that make up the core of our being.

OUR IDENTITY AND LIFE ARE IN CHRIST

We also have a new location. When Christ raised us from the dead, He raised us all the way. That is, after Christ was resurrected, He ascended back into heaven and is seated "at [God's] right hand in the heavenly places" (Eph. 1:20). So if our identity is intrinsically tied with Christ, guess where we are? We are also seated "with Him in the heavenly places" (Eph. 2:6)! That's a spiritual reality, not just wishful thinking. Everything that happened to Christ in His death, burial, and resurrection happened to us spiritually.

Our identification with Christ is so complete that Paul could say, "It is no longer I who live, but Christ lives in me" (Gal. 2:20). That last phrase is loaded with meaning. We must come to grips with the reality that what is happening in this body, through the soul, is the very expression of the life of Christ as He lives in us.

We need to make a crucial clarification here, because most people read this and say, "I get it. Christ is in me and I am in Him." Well, that's true. The most fundamental truth of the Christian life is that Jesus Christ takes up residence within us when we receive Him as Savior. But Galatians 2:20 is saying more than that in terms of our identity as believers. It is not just that Christ is in us, but that He is *living* in us.

The difference between these two is the difference between the standing, or security, we enjoy in Christ, which never changes, and the state or condition of our Christian lives at any particular time, which can be very changeable. The Bible says that because we are in Christ we are "sealed in Him with the Holy Spirit of promise" (Eph. 1:13). This is His seal of security that no one can break and that guarantees us heaven. But Christ does not just want to dwell in you. He wants to live in you—to move in and settle down and fully express Himself through your life.

Allowing Christ to live out His life through you is the fountainhead of growing as a kingdom disciple, for only God working in us by the power of the Holy Spirit can produce lasting growth and change in us.

The tragedy is that a lot of Christians who are going to heaven are not growing in Christ here on earth because they are not allowing Him to be fully at home in their hearts. They treat

Christ the way we treat our guests. We invite our guests to make themselves at home, but we don't usually mean that they're part of the family, free to come and go as they like. We don't want them roaming around the house, looking in our desk and medicine chest, and helping themselves to whatever they find in the kitchen. What we mean by "Make yourself at home" is, "Stay here in this one room and don't mess with anything else."

But to make Jesus Christ at home in your heart, He needs to have the run of the house. Christ indwells every believer, but His presence is more alive and vital in some people than in others because they are allowing Him to live through them and take possession of the whole house.

A lot of us work in the presence of Jesus. We go to church, read books about Jesus, and gather information on Him. But Jesus is saying, "No, this is not enough. I want to express the power of My resurrected life through your body and your spirit. I want to live in you." The Bible says, "We have this treasure in earthen vessels, so that the surpassing greatness of the power will be of God" (2 Cor. 4:7). The purpose of everything we experience is that "the life of Jesus also may be manifested in our body" (v. 10).

QUIT TRYING TO LIVE THE CHRISTIAN LIFE

I've met many frustrated Christians over the years. Many of them tell me they feel frustrated because they are trying so hard to live the Christian life, but it isn't working. If that's your problem, I want to lift a load from your shoulders. Quit trying to live the Christian life. You can't do it. It's impossible. The harder you try to do what God wants you to do, the flatter you will fall on your face.

Jesus is the only Person who has ever lived the Christian life successfully—and the good news is that He offers to live His life in you! God never asked you to be a Christian in your own power. But He does expect you to yield your body to Christ as a living sacrifice (see Rom. 12:1) so He can express His perfect love, power, and holiness through you. That's what it means to be identified with Christ. Anything less than this is like putting your car in neutral and then flooring the gas pedal. You'll make a lot of noise, but you won't get anywhere.

Trying to live the Christian life in your own strength is something like my wishing I could do what Michael Jordan did on the basketball court. Even if Jordan wrote a book about how to do everything he did and I got a copy, it would never work. Why? Because I don't have the hands, the height, or the legs that Michael Jordan had.

Oh, but if it were possible for Mike to say, "I am going to enter your body and empower your hands and legs to fly through the air and dunk a basketball," we would be in business, because that's an entirely different story. Wishing Michael Jordan or some other person could inhabit your body is fiction. Allowing Jesus Christ to express His life through you is reality. He wants to give you everything you need to grow and mature and glorify Him.

THE POWER OF CHRIST WITHIN YOU

Consider 1 Corinthians 1:30: "By [God's] doing you are in Christ Jesus, who became to us wisdom from God, and righteousness and sanctification, and redemption." In other words, when you received Christ you got the whole package. He is your reference point and identity. Through Jesus, there is nothing that is in His will you cannot do (Matt. 19:26). You can declare with Paul, "I can do all things through Him who strengthens me" (Phil. 4:13).

Give me the fingers of Mozart, and there is no musical piece I cannot play. Give me the mind of Einstein, and there is no mathematical formula I cannot unravel. Give me the arms of Hank Aaron, and there is no home run I cannot hit. Give me the life of Jesus Christ, and there is no victory I cannot achieve.

But before you get to thinking that this matter of living as a kingdom disciple is too otherworldly to be practical, I want to take you back to Galatians 2:20. In the last half of this great verse we read, "And the life which I now live in the flesh I live by faith in the Son of God, who loved me and gave Himself up for me."

Living as a kingdom disciple is not just "Let go and let God." This is not a passive relationship in which we sit back and cruise along while Jesus Christ does all the work. He is our life, for sure, but He does not live it apart from us. The new life we received from God operates through our bodies and our personalities. God will not levitate you around so you will always go where He wants you to go. He will be with you as you speak to someone about Christ, but He will not speak through you like a puppeteer using a puppet.

A lot of times we sit around saying things like, "Okay, Lord, I know You want me to read my Bible, so I'm waiting for You to give me a real desire for Your Word." There's nothing wrong with praying for a desire for the Word, but that is more likely to come when you put down the smartphone and pick up your Bible. Again, God is not going to levitate your Bible into your lap and open it to the place He wants you to read. We must work in cooperation with Christ's work in us, and the way we work in cooperation with Jesus Christ is by learning how to operate from the core of our identity, which is our new nature, operating in our soul.

A kingdom disciple must discover the art of operating from his or her spiritually transformed soul rather than merely responding to his or her body. This involves the Holy Spirit's work of stripping us of our self-sufficiency (i.e., brokenness) so that our transformed human spirit dominates the soul, and not vice versa.

Friend, you are not your body. Your body is simply a container for your soul. Your soul is your essence. When a person dies, that soul is what lasts forever. The key to experiencing a true identity with Christ takes place within our soul because our soul is what has been created for eternity.

SIN'S EFFECT ON OUR SOULS

The problem with our souls is that they have been contaminated since birth, making them distorted. Have you ever been to an amusement park and seen the mirrors that make you look fat, super-skinny, tall, short, or crooked? This is what has happened to our souls. To varying degrees, the effects of sin have engrafted themselves into our souls. The soul needs to be fixed, but the difficulty is that the soul cannot fix itself.

Most of the time we are trying to get the soul to fix the soul, but that works just about as well as getting distortion to fix distortion. I call this approach *soul management*. Soul management is when we spend time, energy, and perhaps money trying to make our souls better. We make resolutions and promises that are tied to the soul and its influence on our body. We listen to sermons, cross off our lists, and come up with plans on what we can do to manage our soul.

But God doesn't want us to focus on managing the distortion. Distortion will always be distortion, no matter how well it is managed. What God offers is soul transformation. Sure, we might be able to manage certain parts of our soul for certain lengths of time to certain degrees, but our soul can never deliver itself, make itself better, or set itself free. Only Jesus can do that. Jesus died on the cross not just to take your soul to heaven, but also to deliver your soul in history.

> *God offers soul transformation. Jesus died on the cross to deliver your soul.*

But before deliverance can occur, a second death must occur. This is a willing surrender of your will to the Lord's (first described in chapter 3). Jesus said that if you want to be His disciple, you must "take up" your "cross daily" and follow Him (Luke 9:23). The cross symbolizes an instrument of death. In order for your soul to become fully alive, it must first die, and it will need to die daily.

Every morning when you wake up, don't think about how you can manage your soul. Instead, think about what part of your soul is not in alignment with God and ask Him to let that part die. As long as you try to keep your soul alive, it will continue to be distorted. You will never experience the power and dominion as a kingdom disciple that you were meant to experience by your Creator until your soul dies. The soul within you that needs to die is your self-life, your viewpoint on a matter, the very thoughts that make up your mind.

The Need for the Seed to Grow

Yet not only does your soul need to die, a new life needs to grow within it. This new life first comes to you as a "seed." When you trusted Jesus Christ as your Savior for the forgiveness of your sins, you received what the Bible calls a "seed" that is "imperishable" (1 Peter 1:23). This is your new nature we talked about earlier.

But there are many Christians who have this seed and are still wondering why the Christian life doesn't seem to be working. They try their hand at soul management, but end up being frustrated because the results are only temporary. The reason why the seed is not working to bring about transformation is because the seed has not been allowed to expand.

The expansion of the seed affects the control of the soul. The self-life will continue to rule even though you have the spirit-life within you because the spirit-life is still in seed form. Any time you have a seed and that seed is not planted, it will not express life. The seed has life, but it won't express life. Like a fertilized egg that has become a two-week-old embryo in a mother's womb, this "seed" has all of the DNA within it already for its fullest potential of life. But that two-week-old embryo doesn't express that life as a full-grown baby does just after delivery. That baby is now the result of the seed expanded.

Insight into how to allow the seed to expand comes to us in the book of James. James the apostle writes, "This you know, my beloved brethren. But everyone must be quick to hear, slow to speak and slow to anger" (1:19). You may be wondering how this applies to the spiritual development of a disciple. The answer is: completely.

Notice that James is talking to Christians. He calls them

"beloved brethren." So these verses only apply to those who have trusted Christ for their salvation and are seeking to grow as kingdom disciples. James follows his introduction with a command that is part of the formula to produce growth in you. He says everyone—so that includes all of us—must be quick to hear, slow to speak, and slow to anger.

The question you might be asking is this: quick to hear what? We will find out a few verses later in the passage that we are to be quick to hear God's point of view on a matter. The other question you might be asking is this: slow to speak what? We are to be slow to speak our point of view on a matter. And when God's point of view on a matter differs from our point of view on a matter, then we are told to be slow to anger about it.

However, we often flip it and do the opposite. We are quick to espouse our viewpoint on a matter, and slow to hear His point of view. We are also quick to hear someone else's viewpoint on what they think we should do before we go to God. But God says we should be quick to receive His point of view.

As James continues, we read this: "Therefore, putting aside all filthiness and all that remains of wickedness, in humility receive the word implanted, which is able to save your souls" (v. 21). Notice, the implanted word "is able to save your souls."

"But wait a minute," you say. "These people are already saved. He just called them his 'beloved brethren.' Yet he is still saying that their souls need to be saved." Yes, this is because when you and I trusted Christ for the forgiveness of our sins, our spirits were saved eternally. But our souls were not automatically transformed in history.

When you got saved, you brought your sins and issues to the cross. Jesus saved you for heaven in a flicker of time (i.e., justification). But He saves you on earth progressively (i.e., sanctification). Paul wrote, "The word of the cross is foolishness to those who are perishing, but to us who are being saved it is the power of God" (1 Cor. 1:18). In that verse, we clearly see His reference to us as "being saved," that is, being transformed.

"Receive the word implanted," James wrote, "which is able to save your souls." Thus, remove anything that will interfere with the expansion of the Word implanted. The new nature, which is consistent with the Word of God, has been implanted in your soul in seed form. God says to receive it, or welcome it within.

One reason we are not experiencing victory as kingdom disciples even though we desire to do better is because the implanted seed has not been welcomed into our souls. God says if you will accept what has been implanted within you, it will deliver your soul. But you must actively receive it, not contradict it or ignore it. This means that as kingdom disciples who want to continue in spiritual growth, we *must* maintain lifestyles of repentance. As James says in 1:21, we are to lay aside all evil. Repentance is the inner resolve and determination to turn from sin and to turn in obedience to God. Since sin breaks fellowship with God, repentance is the means by which that broken relationship is restored, freeing the Holy Spirit to activate the life in the seed so that spiritual growth and intimacy takes place (1 John 1:5–9). This repentance is the ongoing response of the believer who is seeking to become a kingdom disciple.

The Need for the Word to Nourish

The implanted word can be best illustrated by comparing it to a fertilized egg in the womb of a woman. To develop, the fertilized egg must receive nourishment from an outside source.

The woman eats, and the nutrients from her food travel to the umbilical cord where they enable the fertilized egg to develop into a growing baby.

Just as the fertilized egg requires nourishment to develop into the baby it will one day be upon delivery, the seed that has been implanted in us also requires nourishment. The written Word of God must reach into the depth of our soul, where the implanted Word abides with the imperishable seed so that seed may expand and the life of Christ is expressed.

The only tool designed to expand the seed located in the soul is the Word of God. There are no other tools. Sunday morning preaching, in and of itself, is not a tool. Inspirational books, in and of themselves, are not a tool. Even topical studies, by themselves, are not a tool. While these things are good in our personal growth and development, they cannot be substituted for the soul welcoming the very Word of God. You must engage with, study, memorize, meditate on, and seek to understand and apply God's Word—daily. You must also receive it.

Some of you reading this may have been going to church for years. You may have been reading your Bible for years. But your soul has not changed. Or it changes for a while and then goes back to how it was before. Why isn't it working for you? The answer to your question is found in the word "receive." It is possible to have the Word implanted but to still have not received it. The word "receive" means to "welcome," that is, to embrace it with a decision to obey.

When we welcome the Word of God, it goes to work in our souls. Hebrews describes Scripture's effects this way: "The word of God is living and active and sharper than any two-edged sword, and piercing as far as the division of soul and spirit, of both joints and marrow, and able to judge the thoughts and intentions of the heart" (4:12).

The Word of God is alive. The Greek word used there is *logos*. It means the living word. "In the beginning was the Word, and the Word was with God, and the Word was God" (John 1:1). It is the energized, life-giving Word of God.

The Bible calls this Word food for the soul. Just like you have food for the body that supplies proper nutrition to enable your body to function well, there is also food for the soul. The Bible is to the soul what food is to the body. Jesus said that we should not "live on bread alone, but on every word that proceeds out of the mouth of God" (Matt. 4:4).

THE WORD'S EFFECT ON OUR SOUL AND SPIRIT

The book of Hebrews tells us that when this food reaches where it needs to in our soul, it pierces as far as the division of our soul and spirit so that we can differentiate between what is from God and what is from us. But in order for it to do that, it needs to be received and welcomed within. To be received means it has to reach further than just your ears during a Sunday sermon. The purpose of the sermon is to inspire you into a deeper personal study in the Word on the subject preached. You must do the work of discipleship in your own soul. No one else can do it for you.

What is the soul? It is your essence. It is your mind, emotions, and will. What is the spirit? That is the divine nature, the seed He has implanted in you—your new nature. When the Word gets down to the level that it needs to, it is going to make a distinction between what is you and what is God.

The Word of God will divide what is your life and what is

God's life. What are your thoughts and what are God's thoughts? What are your feelings and what are God's feelings? What is your choice and what is God's choice? The Word of God is going to make a distinction between the two.

Remember, Scripture tells us that "the heart is more deceitful than all else" (Jer. 17:9). That is why we need Scripture, "for the word of God . . . is able to judge the thoughts and intentions of the heart" (Heb. 4:12). We need God's Word to discern what is truth in our hearts and what is flesh. Just as the heart is vital to pumping blood to every part of your body, God's Word is vital and has power when it reaches your heart.

You may read this book and it works its way to your head, and you say, "Tony, I understand what you're talking about." Or it works its way to your emotions and you say, "Yes, I feel what you are writing about." Or it works its way to your will and you say, "I know a decision that I need to make."

But if it doesn't get to the heart, it hasn't arrived at its destination. And if it hasn't arrived at its destination, then it hasn't been received.

As the seed expands in your soul, it will begin to dominate your thoughts, feelings, and will so that actions that reflect the viewpoint of God will become natural to you in your daily life. That's the difference. They won't just be reactions that you have based on a sermon, chapter, or devotional you read that morning. You will live as a kingdom disciple naturally, organically—fluidly.

> *Be quick to hear God's viewpoint on a matter. Be slow to speak your viewpoint on a matter.*

But in order to get to that point, you need to receive the Word implanted at a level where it is able to judge the thoughts and intentions of your heart. Remember:

Be quick to hear. Hear what? *God's viewpoint on a matter.*
Be slow to speak. Speak what? *Your viewpoint on a matter.*

And be slow to anger when His viewpoint is different than yours, your parents, your friends, and your coworkers.

God says don't get mad when you don't like what you hear. Because God's not trying to be popular right now. He's trying to set you free by saving your soul. When the Word of God dwells richly in your soul, you will not have to force yourself to live with your identity in Christ. Christ, who is the living Word (John 1:1), will be your identity naturally. The life of a kingdom disciple is a life that results from inner transformation based on the power of the Spirit enabling the power of the Word to so fully link you with Christ that you reflect Him in all you do.

THE BEGINNING POINT:
OUR POSITION WITH JESUS

Colossians 3:1 is crucial to the process of replacing our viewpoint with God's viewpoint. Paul wrote, "Since, then, you have been raised with Christ, set your hearts on things above, where Christ is, seated at the right hand of God" (NIV). The solution to the problem of living as a kingdom disciple is not down here on earth. The beginning point of our identity is our spiritual position with Christ.

How do you "set your heart on things above"? You seek the things above with all that is in you. The Greek word for "set your heart" is a term used frequently in Scripture to refer to seeking, looking, or searching earnestly. We find it in the words of Jesus:

- "But seek first His kingdom." (Matt. 6:33)
- "Ask, and it will be given to you; seek, and you will find." (Matt. 7:7)
- "Why is it that you were looking for Me? Did you not know that I had to be in My Father's house?" (Luke 2:49)
- "And do not seek what you will eat and what you will drink, and do not keep worrying." (Luke 12:29 NIV)
- "Or what woman, if she has ten silver coins and loses one coin, does not light a lamp and sweep the house and search carefully until she finds it?" (Luke 15:8)
- "For the Son of Man has come to seek and to save that which was lost." (Luke 19:10)

Setting our "heart on things above," we are to earnestly and consistently seek out His perspective on every issue in our lives, even when that perspective contradicts our own. We are not to be like the apostle Peter who invoked God's name in the use of well-intentioned human logic designed to protect his master from suffering and the cross (Matt. 16:21–28). Jesus rebuked his thinking as having its source in Satan, because it was not consistent with the plan of God. It is in God's revealed truth and not our human perspective that we find the keys to living victoriously and ruling authoritatively as kingdom disciples.

So what are the major components of who we are to be and what we are to do in Christ, as summarized in what Jesus calls the two great commandments? We are to love God and love others. Do these two things and all else will align under God's rule. I realize I am revisiting what we looked at in chapter 4 on our commitment and its cost, but we as the body of Christ have gotten so far removed from these two primary laws of love that revisiting it is necessary.

When your heart and your mind regularly seek to live out the essence of these two commandments of loving God and loving others, you are living as a kingdom disciple. Keep returning your heart and your mind to these two truths and the rest will fall into place.

Change your mindset from earth's values to heaven's, and you'll start living as a kingdom disciple.

Remember, though, the desire to seek—as in the examples given for that term in Scripture—is typically motivated by emotions. It requires that you regularly return your heart *and* mind to the biblical definition of love and seek to live it out. Remember also that love includes kindness, gentleness, self-control, humility, contentment, patience, forgiveness, hope, and belief. Love is truth.

Jesus made a very revealing statement one day. "You will know the truth, and the truth will make you free" (John 8:32). Stated another way, if you're a Christian, the fact of your new identity in Christ is true whether you have grasped it or not. True reality for you is located in the attributes found in heavenly places, not on earth. Once you change your mindset from earth's values to heaven's, you'll start living as a kingdom disciple. And you will begin to experience the benefits of your identity in Christ, beginning with His peace.

The apostle Paul wrote, "The peace of God, which surpasses

all comprehension, will guard your hearts and your minds in Christ Jesus" (Phil. 4:7). That word "guard" means to do sentry duty, to stand guard. In Colossians 3:15, Paul said God's peace will "rule" in our hearts. Could you use a little peace in your life right now? I think we all probably could.

The Holy Spirit allows this peace—and joy—to rule in your heart when your heart and identity are hidden with Christ, in God, and reflect His character and attributes as a kingdom disciple (Rom. 14:17).

CHAPTER 6

A Deep Intimacy

Many longtime married couples will agree that intimacy is one of the first elements of a marriage to deteriorate if it is not cultivated. That's ironic because for most young couples in a serious dating or courtship relationship, it's this very quality of intimacy that makes everything so special and so exciting.

Before marriage, there is the romantic and emotional intimacy of being together—sharing thoughts and dreams and laughter and just delighting in each other's presence. The intimacy continues even when the two are apart as they talk on the phone or text each other and get lost in their thoughts of the other person. And even in a sexually pure premarital relationship, there is the intimacy of an arm around the shoulder and a kiss, or a hand held gently.

If you dated in the days before seat belts, you remember sitting as close as possible to your beloved. In fact, in those days you could tell when a couple wasn't getting along, because the girl would be sitting as close to the passenger door as possible. Another thing that is usually true of those early, exhilarating days of first love is that relationship is dominant over performance.

By that I mean the girl might say, "Honey, I need to tell you I'm not exactly the best cook in the world."

He didn't hear a word she said. He's so entranced by her eyes and the adorable way she talks that her cooking ability is totally irrelevant to him. It works the other way too. The guy may have an entry-level job, or be in school and be barely able to afford gas, a burger, and a movie. But she treasures the ticket stub from their first date like it was a diamond engagement ring.

And then when a couple comes together in the sacred bond of marriage, their joy is multiplied as they discover the pleasure and intimacy of a committed, one-flesh physical relationship.

Now the honeymoon stage of marriage comes to an end, and that's okay, because it isn't meant to last. But while the newness of a relationship may wear off, the intimacy doesn't have to fade. In fact, God's purpose for a kingdom marriage is that a couple's intimacy—true oneness of heart and spirit and body—should deepen and become richer with the passing of time.

Intimacy is one of the greatest delights and blessings that two people in a close relationship can have. The capacity to draw close to another person and share your lives in such a way that you know each other through and through is part of the image of God that we bear as emotional and relational human beings.

Now let me ask you a question. If God designed us with a deep need and deep desire for intimacy in our human relationships, and if intimacy reflects God's image within us, what do you suppose God is seeking in His relationship with us? You guessed it—He wants a close, committed relationship. Yet, unfortunately, God is far too often the jilted love in our one-sided relationships with Him. But He desires the intimacy of a close relationship with you.

The rest of God's creation performs for Him, but the intimacy of relationship with Him is reserved for the people who know Christ as their Savior and have a new identity in Him. We often hear the question asked, "If you knew that God Himself was waiting at a Starbucks to talk and spend time with you, would you rush to meet with Him?" I'm sure the answer is yes, and you would probably skip ordering a coffee! Friend, God does desire, even yearns for, an intimate spiritual relationship with you. Yes, you!

Three passages of Scripture teach this truth, a vital part of your life as a kingdom disciple. It's vital because true intimacy motivates us in all we do. When you love your spouse truly, your spouse doesn't have to ask you to call, take out the trash, get the laundry done, or all of the necessary duties of life. You do it naturally. Not only that, but two people who know each other intimately are free to be themselves around each other. They feel no pressure to prove anything by trying to meet a performance standard or by trying to be someone they aren't. So if your deep desire is to live victoriously as a kingdom disciple, I recommend that you begin developing an intimate, rich, spiritually satisfying love relationship with Jesus Christ.

THE PASSION OF INTIMACY

Intimacy definitely involves passion, of which physical passion is just one component. That's usually the aspect we think of first, but it's not as important as spiritual intimacy. Here's my definition of passion: an all-consuming drive to get closer to, and to know more fully, the person with whom we wish to be intimate. So our relationship with Christ as His disciples should be marked by a never-ending passion to know Him better and draw closer to Him. Paul had that kind of passion to know Christ intimately. We know because the apostle told us so in his classic statement of relationship versus performance in Philippians 3:4–14.

The context here is important, because the chapter begins with a warning about "dogs" and "the false circumcision" (Phil. 3:2). These were the "Judaizers," those who were trying to make the Philippians focus on rule-keeping rather than on their relationship with Christ. Their passion was upholding rules. In contrast, Paul wrote that the power of the Christian life is in knowing Christ (v. 10).

Philippians 3:3 offers a concise description of life as a kingdom disciple. "We are the true circumcision, who worship in the Spirit of God and glory in Christ Jesus and put no confidence in the flesh." What a declaration of the value of the person of Christ over religious performance. The only answer for the flesh is to nail it to the cross of Christ. Anyone who is confident of being able to live for Christ in the energy of the flesh is doomed to spiritual defeat.

In verse 4, Paul began a digression that took him through verse 6, a review of his credentials as a "Jew of Jews," one of the brightest young stars in the contemporary Jewish world. The argument was straightforward and irrefutable. If fleshly standards of performance, even religious passion, could win God's favor, Paul would have been at the head of the line to get into heaven. The man had a résumé no one could match:

> [I was] circumcised the eighth day, of the nation of Israel, of the tribe of Benjamin, a Hebrew of Hebrews; as to the Law, a Pharisee; as to zeal, a persecutor of the church; as to the righteousness which is in the Law, found blameless. (Phil. 3:5–6)

Nothing was missing in Paul's religious upbringing. He came from the right family, and he had all the little medals for perfect synagogue attendance. He had been made a part of the covenant nation of Israel through the rite of circumcision. Paul also came from the right side of the tracks. The men of Benjamin's tribe were warriors, the ones who stayed faithful when the rest of the nation turned left on God. Paul had all the ingredients to be a Jew among Jews, at the top of the pack.

This brilliant Jewish man put his advantages to work. He became a Pharisee, the pinnacle of the religious hierarchy. He studied the Law. He may have memorized the Pentateuch, the five books of Moses. He could say he scrupulously kept the Law, and when a sacrifice needed to be offered, he was there with it.

And Paul didn't do all of this with a yawn, either. He was so on fire for his Pharisaic Judaism that he said, "Let me round up these Christians. I'll hunt all of them down. If you want someone to stamp out this new cult, I'm your man" (see Acts 9:1–2). There was only one thing Paul was missing. He didn't know Christ, so all of his credentials were useless before God. This idea is hard for people today to accept because our entire culture is driven by performance. How well you do determines your raises and promotions at work, your acceptance in many social circles, and maybe even your acceptance at home.

But spiritual reality hit Paul between the eyes that day when he hit the dirt on his way to Damascus as Jesus stopped him and saved him (Acts 9:3–9). Now Paul could say, "But whatever things were gain to me, those things I have counted as loss for the sake of Christ" (Phil. 3:7). When Paul met Jesus on the Damascus road, he had to leave all his religious pride and performance lying there in the dust. He had to face the same realization all sinners must face, that the only way to heaven is a Person, not a performance sheet.

What I want you to see is the extent of Paul's passion to know Christ intimately—because, remember, this is all heading toward a climactic statement in verse 10. Paul said in effect, "I met a Person who will take me to heaven, and I'm still getting to know this Person who makes me powerful and victorious on earth." The power to live for Christ comes from knowing the person of Christ and from receiving the righteousness that comes only through faith in Him (Phil. 3:9).

> *Paul had to face what all sinners must face, that the only way to heaven is a Person, not a performance sheet.*

What you need to see throughout this passage is that Paul gladly left behind his pursuit of superstardom in Judaism because of his passion to know Christ with the kind of intimacy that transcended every other relationship.

"THAT I MAY KNOW HIM"

This brings us to Philippians 3:10. If you need a verse to build your life around, this is it. If you want a pursuit to focus the rest of your life on, there's no better one than this. "That I may know Him and the power of His resurrection and the fellowship of His sufferings, being conformed to His death."

Kingdom disciples pursue knowing Christ intimately.

Paul once made a very interesting statement in regard to his knowledge of Christ. The apostle said, "Even though we have known Christ according to the flesh, yet now we know Him in this way no longer" (2 Cor. 5:16). Before his conversion, Paul knew about Christ in the sense that he had heard about this Man Jesus and perhaps had even seen Him once. But after becoming a Christian, Paul truly came to know the Lord, and his previous casual knowledge was erased because he became a brand-new creation (v. 17). Paul came face-to-face with resurrection power.

Why is it that some Christians have victory while others are defeated? The answer isn't in their circumstances, because victorious Christians and defeated Christians face basically the same kinds of trials. The answer isn't in who goes to church more often or who reads the Bible more. The answer is that victorious Christians know Christ more intimately, and thus experience His resurrection power, the kingdom authority that is transferred to kingdom disciples.

A lot of us would like to put a period after the phrase "the power of His resurrection" in Philippians 3:10. But if we are going to know Christ with the kind of intimacy that draws us close, we must know Him in "the fellowship of His sufferings, being conformed to His death."

We are called to share in Christ's sufferings. For Paul, having fellowship with Christ in His sufferings meant severe persecution, numerous hardships, and finally martyrdom. But it also meant a special kind of intimacy and authority with the Lord that can't be known any other way. If you have ever suffered deeply with another person, you know what I'm talking about. We'll never be truly intimate with somebody else if we say to that person, "I only want to share the good times with you. Keep your suffering to yourself."

So many believers today want to know the five things they can do to achieve spiritual victory and exercise spiritual authority as a disciple or the four steps to peace. That's the American way. Just give me a list of things to do, and I'll knock myself out doing them. Don't misunderstand. Nothing I am saying about performance-oriented discipleship is meant to imply that we don't have to do anything as Christians. God has prepared us to do good works (Eph. 2:10). And there may well be four or five things we could either stop doing, or start doing, to strengthen our life with Christ.

The problem is that we attribute to our lists a power they don't have. Suppose someone says to me, "Tony, give me a list of five things I can do to be a better Christian." So I give him a list of the basic stuff, like reading his Bible and spending time in prayer, and then I call him two weeks later to see how it's going. "Not really any better," he tells me. "I already knew about the things on the list. I just can't seem to pull them off consistently."

This imaginary person's problem is our problem too. We know what to do. The issue is where we get the power to do what we know. The Bible says the power comes in the relationship. The power comes when the living word, Jesus Christ, reaches the implanted word in our soul. The power comes through abiding in Christ.

ABIDING IN THE VINE

Jesus spoke the words in John 15 in the upper room just before His crucifixion, probably the most intimate setting we are told about in Scripture. With His disciples close around Him, and John leaning on Him (John 13:23), Jesus said, "I am the true vine, and My Father is the vinedresser. Every branch in Me that does not bear fruit, He takes away; and every branch that bears fruit, He prunes it so that it may bear more fruit" (15:1–2).

Jesus used a familiar illustration to make His point. The disciples knew all about vines and fruit. The question was, then, how were they to produce the fruit that God desired?

Jesus continued, "Abide in Me, and I in you. As the branch cannot bear fruit of itself unless it abides in the vine, so neither can you unless you abide in Me. I am the vine, you are the branches; he who abides in Me and I in him, he bears much fruit, for apart from Me you can do nothing" (John 15:4–5). Fruit has three key characteristics. First, it always bears the character of the tree of which it is a part (pear trees don't produce apples). Second, fruit is always visible. Third, fruit exists for the benefit of others. Fruit that eats itself is rotten. Therefore, kingdom disciples make disciples, producing fruit in the lives of others (v. 8).

Authority in prayer is the practical manifestation and result of the transfer of kingdom authority. Jesus says that those believers who possess an intimacy with him get heaven's response to their prayers (John 15:7). Heaven obligates itself to respond to believers who function as kingdom disciples when they invoke God's presence in the affairs of this life. For kingdom disciples, seeing the supernatural operating in the natural is not to be an occasional event. Answered prayer for kingdom disciples is part of the legal right bequeathed to those who legitimately exercise the authority granted to them based on the level of their relational commitment to the Savior.

The key is in your connection to Christ. As branches you bear fruit, but the life-giving substance flows to you from the Vine. Anytime you try to produce fruit on your own, it's going to lack the necessary nutrients and power to produce fruit that lasts.

"Abiding in Christ" is another name for intimacy with Christ.

> "Abiding in Christ" is another name for intimacy with Christ.

Christ wants to express His life through you, which comes through your attachment to Him. If your prayer life is just a matter of shooting up panicked emergency petitions when you're in trouble, you're missing this intimacy. If you have your devotions in the morning so you can get them out of the way and get on with your day, you don't understand abiding. If church is just your weekly "time with God," you won't bear fruit.

This is because abiding means just what it says. It means to remain, to stay, to keep the connection strong. It means you can take a deep breath and just get to know Jesus. It takes away all the self-induced struggle.

A young woman in our church, after years of smoking, decided she wanted to kick the habit. She tried every stop-smoking product on the market, but nothing worked. Finally, she decided that instead of focusing on all the things she was doing to quit smoking, she would focus on being in God's presence and getting to know Him. Within thirty days, she had quit smoking because of the power of His presence. When you are close to Jesus Christ, you find what you need to overcome the struggles you face. Not only that, you will experience doors opening for you that you never could have opened on your own.

The story is told that a bulldog and a poodle were arguing one day. The bulldog was making fun of the poodle, calling him a weak little runt who couldn't do anything. Then the bulldog said, "I challenge you to a contest. Let's see who can open the back door of their house the fastest and get inside."

The bulldog was thinking he would turn the doorknob with his powerful jaws and open the door, while the poodle was too small even to reach the knob on his back door.

But to the bulldog's surprise, the poodle said, "I can get inside my house faster than you can. I accept the challenge."

So with the poodle watching, the bulldog ran to the back door of his house and jumped up to the doorknob. He got his teeth and paws around the knob and tried to turn it, but he couldn't get enough of a grip on the knob to turn it. He finally had to quit in exhaustion.

Now it was the poodle's turn at his back door. "Go ahead, you can't do it either," the bulldog growled, trying to soothe his wounded pride. The poodle went to the door and scratched a couple of times. The owner of the home not only opened the door, but lovingly picked the poodle up in his arms and carried him inside.

The difference was in the relationship. Some of us are bulldog Christians. It's all grunting and growling and trying, when Christ wants us to come close to Him. Get close to Christ as His disciple and He will amaze you with what He will do both in and through you.

THE PROCESS OF INTIMACY

The title of this section may sound unusual, because intimacy seems like one of those things that should just happen spontaneously, without any real direction. Wrong. Ask any married couple if deep, satisfying emotional, spiritual, and physical intimacy happens magically, with no effort on the part of either spouse. They will tell you it doesn't work that way.

There is a process to intimacy with Jesus, and we looked at it in the previous chapter when we touched on receiving "the word implanted, which is able to save your souls" (James 1:21). Jesus added this next statement when He was talking to His disciples about abiding. He included a very important element when He said, "If you abide in Me and My words abide in you, ask whatever you wish, and it will be done for you" (John 15:7).

He says that if we abide, or remain, in Him and keep His words in us, then we can ask whatever we want and it will be done. We can ask to be set free from an addiction, wrong attitude, oppressive relationship, or anything that is contrary to His will. We can ask for that promotion, dream, or destiny. But here's the question. How do I get His words to remain in me? How do I get His words to reach deep down into that level we talked about earlier where the seed has been planted? Where it will make a difference so that I will become what I was redeemed to be?

The epistle of James answers that question. After we have received God's Word, James tells us to be "doers of the word" instead of those who are just "hearers." He explains why this is necessary:

> For if anyone is a hearer of the word and not a doer, he is like a man who looks at his natural face in a mirror; for once he has looked at himself and gone away, he has immediately forgotten what kind of person he was. But one who looks intently at the perfect law, the law of liberty, and abides by it, not having become a forgetful hearer but an effectual doer, this man will be blessed in what he does. (James 1:23–25)

The word "man" used in that passage is the Greek word for "male." Typically a man looks at himself in a mirror briefly and then goes away, forgetting what he just saw. In contrast, women spend more time before the mirror, paying close attention to their appearance.

James says we should approach the Scriptures as a woman looks at a mirror—looking at the details. We are to take our time to meditate on verses, until the Holy Spirit affects our souls with the Bible's transforming truths. James says to "look intently" at the perfect law. He says to let the Word of God liberate you by not being a forgetful hearer but an effectual doer of it. In order to become an effectual doer of the Scriptures, they need to flow naturally out of you.

For that to happen, a relationship with the living Word, Jesus, must be established. A casual reading or hearing of the Scriptures will never work. Hearing a sermon or even reading a book written about the Word can wind up being a waste of time. You may have heard it or read it, but the Word is unusable because it wasn't allowed to abide, remain, and expand into what it was created to be. When you abide in God's Word and depend on the Holy Spirit, spiritual transformation is inevitable (2 Cor. 3:17–18).

ABIDING: SPENDING TIME IN THE RIGHT SETTING

James writes that you must look intently. Jesus said, "If you continue in My word, then you are truly disciples of Mine" (John 8:31). It's like someone recharging their cellphone at the end of the day. When you plug your cellphone into the charger, you let it hang out there so it can abide with the electricity needed to power it. If you let the phone stay away too long, all the power is lost.

You say that you've got this problem in your life and you have prayed and asked God to deliver you but He hasn't? Well, do you know how it is when you have dirty dishes that have been sitting out for a while and things get hard and crusty? What do you do? You soak them. You let them hang out in some hot water.

After they hang out long enough—abiding in the water—what you would have had to scrape off can now slide off because it's been abiding in an environment designed to address it. In a way, abiding is spending time in the right setting, to renew and recharge.

Remember what we talked about in the last chapter? You have an implant in you. You have a seed. It is your new nature. When you abide with Jesus—His words, His perspective, His viewpoint on a matter—that word connects with the seed that is already in you and it begins to expand. Your soul must give way then to the domination of the spirit as it grows.

That means your soul no longer has control over you. It no longer speaks the final word. Here's how you'll know when the seed is growing and the spirit is taking over. You'll know because the changes that take place inside of you will become natural to you. You won't have to force peace. You won't have to force kindness. You won't have to force graciousness or create false hope. You won't have to check off your obedience list. Or feign respect to your family member, coworker, or boss. It will just come out of you naturally because of the expansion of the seed within you—the new life identified with Jesus Christ. You will be exercising kingdom authority as a kingdom disciple.

This seed—this relationship and identification with Jesus Christ and His words—will let your soul know: "Hey, soul, that's not who we are anymore. We don't talk like that. We don't look at that. We don't treat people like that. We don't drink like that.

We don't complain like that. We don't give up like that. We don't manipulate like that. We don't worry like that. That's not who we are now."

By identifying with Christ through an intimate, abiding relationship of fellowshiping in His sufferings, conforming to His character, and abiding in His words, you can live as a victorious kingdom disciple. And not just for a week. Or a few months. But for always.

CHAPTER 7

A Steady Increase

Have you ever taken the time to open an album of your baby and toddler pictures and get a glimpse of what life was like for you when you were very young? "Throwback Thursday" on social media gives many people an opportunity to share these photos with friends and family. It's fun to see each other when we were younger.

But what would life be like for you if you had stayed that age forever? If you had never learned to eat on your own, dress yourself, or make your own decisions? Most of us, I'm sure, were very cute as a baby and a toddler, but I'm also sure we would not want to have stayed that way. That's because while being a baby is a normal, necessary part of life, it isn't the goal. The goal of every individual is to grow and mature into a functioning, contributing adult.

Can you imagine a country made up only of babies and toddlers? That country wouldn't last long at all. Nor would it have much of an economy.

Now, can you imagine the body of Christ made up only of spiritual babies and toddlers? Again, that's not a pleasant situation. God is not satisfied simply that His children are born again of the Spirit. He is not satisfied merely that we accepted Jesus Christ as our personal sin-bearer. He desires to see His baby believers grow up to become mature followers who can represent their King and exercise kingdom authority. This process of moving from spiritual infancy to spiritual maturity is called discipleship. The goal is that once you are spiritually mature, you then disciple someone else that they may grow in their faith as well. The author of the book of Hebrews spent some considerable time talking to Christians in his day about this issue. Some of the believers he was writing to had been saved for thirty years. Yet even with all of that time, they were not spiritually mature. They still needed to nurse on the milk of truth rather than apply and digest the meat. That's why the writer challenged, corrected, and pretty much insisted that they begin to progress in their spiritual development. He urged them, as I'm urging you through this book, to become kingdom disciples.

The author of Hebrews introduces the concept of spiritual growth this way:

> Concerning him we have much to say, and it is hard to explain, since you have become dull of hearing. For though by this time you ought to be teachers, you have need again for someone to teach you the elementary principles of the oracles of God, and you have come to need milk and not solid food. For everyone who partakes only of milk is not accustomed to the word of righteousness, for he is an infant. But solid food is for the mature, who because of practice have their senses trained to discern good and evil. (Heb. 5:11–14)

He specifically used the word "mature." Maturity means to have reached a place in your life where you are responsible. We typically tie the term "responsibility" with "maturity." It does not always delineate a status of age. After all, you have probably either said or heard someone say to an adult, "It's time for you to grow up." Now, this person may be in their thirties, forties, or even older. But the comment of "growing up" is not referring to growing in age. It refers to growing in maturity. They are not functioning in a responsible, wise manner. I've counseled enough people to have heard this phrase far more than I ever care to.

Maturity has nothing to do with the number of birthdays a person has had. It has everything to do with a person's mindset and wisdom; maturity shows itself in self-control and responsibility. Similarly, spiritual maturity does not automatically come to a believer because he or she attends church for a designated number of years. Or because they put in time at a Bible study, small group, or even in their own personal devotions. Spiritual maturity has everything to do with a believer who is consistently operating underneath the rule of God in every area of life. The person makes each decision from a kingdom perspective rather than a worldly or even personal perspective. He is able to consistently carry out spiritually based decisions.

Although nobody is a perfect Christian, maturity as a kingdom disciple does refer to consistency. It means you are consistently operating based on God's framework, appealing to His spiritual wisdom in all you do. Now, keep in mind this is not our natural way of thinking or living. It doesn't come to us easily or organically to live with "the mind of Christ" (1 Cor. 2:16). Just like a baby cannot be expected to explain his or her decisions, a disciple must grow into the adoption of a kingdom mindset—a Christ-centered point of view.

You are a mature disciple when you are able to consistently apply divine truth to your day-to-day decisions. Spiritual maturity has nothing to do with how long you have been saved. It has everything to do with how much you have developed after having been saved. God has far too many thirty-year-old infants in His church. And you are well aware of how much time, effort, and additional support an adult who cannot care for himself requires strictly from a physical standpoint. This also carries over into the local church. Much of the mess we face—the fires we have to put out in our churches, and the pains we experience—are simply because of the overabundance of spiritually anemic believers.

The Rate of Growth

When Paul wrote to the believers in Corinth, he chided them for their lack of spiritual maturity. These individuals had been saved for five years, but they were still acting, thinking, and talking like spiritual infants. We read his rebuking words in 1 Corinthians 3:1–3:

> And I, brethren, could not speak to you as to spiritual men,
> but as to men of flesh, as to infants in Christ. I gave you milk
> to drink, not solid food; for you were not yet able to receive it.
> Indeed, even now you are not yet able, for you are still fleshly.
> For since there is jealousy and strife among you, are you not
> fleshly, and are you not walking like mere men?

Paul first visited Corinth in AD 50. This is when he planted the church. We can call it Corinth Bible Fellowship. But Paul wrote the letter now known as 1 Corinthians in AD 55, five years later. Within those five years, Paul had expected these believers to have become mature disciples. Instead he found them operating on the secular human level of thought. He did not see them flowing on a spiritual level.

While this benchmark of five years applies to the church at Corinth, we know that it is even possible to become spiritually mature faster than that. In fact, Paul himself did. But this benchmark means it definitely shouldn't take more than five years.

So what can be said of believers today who have been church members for decades, and yet still operate from the mindset of the flesh rather than the rule of God over their lives? They are Christians, but they are not kingdom disciples. And Paul's disappointment is only a fraction of what our Lord must feel when He witnesses His children failing to progress in spiritual growth.

You know how proud parents are when they witness the physical growth of their child. In fact, many parents will even mark that growth on the inside wall of a closet, or a door frame. Perhaps more pleasing is when their son or daughter grows in wisdom and the ability to make right choices. How must God feel to go year after year in witnessing the walk and choices of His children, only to experience them remaining stagnant in growth—or worse yet, even living in a backslidden condition?

> *Believers who operate from the mindset of the flesh are Christians, but they are not kingdom disciples.*

We all know that the rate at which an object moves will

determine its arrival. If I were to set out from the church where I pastor and walk to downtown Dallas, I would arrive there later than if I set out from the same place and drove. Similarly, our Christian development toward becoming a mature disciple is impacted by the rate at which we apply ourselves toward that growth.

If one believer chooses to grow by only attending church, and another adds a twenty-minute devotional time, those decisions will impact each person's speed of growth. If a third believer aggressively studies God's Word, whether formally at a Bible school or informally through the myriad of discipleship materials and courses now available to so many people online, as well as through additional reading, that person will often grow more quickly than the other two.

A fourth person who not only aggressively studies but also seeks to increasingly apply the principles from the studying will grow faster still. And like a log in a fireplace that burns brighter and more fully when other logs are there with it, a person who studies, applies, and joins with like-minded believers to discuss and admonish will progress even more quickly.

The speed of which you move over the time you use determines the distance you cover. This is true in physical movement; it is also true in spiritual movement.

So why were the members of Corinth Bible Fellowship not progressing in their discipleship process? They were not willing to hear and apply the principles of God's Word. The writer of Hebrews gives us insight into this reality when we read in Hebrews 5:11, "Concerning him we have much to say, and it is hard to explain, since you have become dull of hearing." Like the recipients of this letter, the Corinthian believers had been "dull of hearing." The word "dull" means to be lazy or sluggish. It also can mean to struggle to the point of giving up. What it boils down to is that the reason there was a lack of spiritual development and growth was that the believers were lazy.

That reality makes me sigh. I sigh because there is so much to be gained in life and eternity by living as a mature kingdom disciple. But because people don't always readily identify these gains, laziness often creeps in. It's like would-be exercisers who see the visible benefits their friends receive through exercise yet are too lazy to exercise themselves.

One of my greatest burdens as a pastor lies in this area of discipleship. It is my life passion to study and teach God's Word but, more often than I'd like to admit, I've run into a church member by Tuesday who can't remember even the subject of the Sunday message. I've seen too many walk away from a Sunday sermon "dull of hearing" (Heb. 5:11), too lazy to revisit what was taught, dig deeper on their own, apply the principles, and do the difficult work of spiritual exercise. Becoming a kingdom disciple is not automatic.

> *There is so much to be gained in life and eternity by living as a mature kingdom disciple.*

Anything you or I achieve in life is because we invested in it. If you graduated from high school or college, it was because you attended, completed the assignments, paid the fees, and grew in your development. You invested. Same thing for your career. If you have risen in the ranks of your career, it is not because you sat back and were lazy. Things that happen in life that you progress in and get better at doing happen because there is an investment—an investment of time, energy, thought, money, actions, and more.

For a number of years I served as a chaplain in the National Football League. I can guarantee that not one single player on the football teams I served was there because he was lazy. Even if a player had worked out consistently and developed great muscle strength, yet had refused to apply what he heard from his coach on how to use those skills, he would not have remained on the team. It required a significant amount of personal investment, sacrifice—even pain—for the NFL players to play on the level that they did.

Too many believers today want the miracles, blessings, and power of Christianity, but are not willing to put in the investment to grow and mature. In other words, they want the perks and benefits that come with playing in the NFL without the effort and dedication it takes to get to that level.

A few years ago I visited the NFL offices in New York City for a meeting about some mentoring materials we had created for coaches to use with athletes. While waiting on my meeting to start, the NFL commissioner, Roger Goodell, walked by, along with his team of security. He nodded my way and we said a brief hello. As he continued walking, I noticed he carried an air of intent resolve. He strode purposefully, his face serious. It dawned on me as I watched him head into the elevators, presumably to his office, how much weight must be on that one man. After all, what the NFL has managed to accomplish is nothing short of staggering. Maintaining and growing that accomplishment is surely a heavy burden.

Despite its very rocky start—when stations wouldn't even broadcast a game—over the years the NFL has done a tremendous job from a business standpoint of surpassing baseball as America's pastime. Professional football has also eclipsed pro basketball. Today pro football commands the highest prices for advertisements of any sport. The 2017 Super Bowl had over 111 million viewers, making it the third-highest-watched event in the history of television.

Did this growth come about by chance? Never. Just as the professional athletes must work out strenuously so their bodies can play at the ultimate level, the NFL administrators (including Goodell), marketers, and PR personnel have spent years massaging the sport's image and engaging its fan base, to achieve their dominance.

Success is not a result of luck or chance. Success always comes by way of sweat, effort, skill, and diligence. Similarly, success in our spiritual lives will not happen to us by osmosis because we happen to attend a service here or there, or we keep a Bible on our bed stand and read a verse a day to keep the devil away. Spiritual growth, success, and dominance over the enemies of the world, the flesh, and the devil will only come about through dedication, effort, sacrifice, wisdom, and application. Spiritual maturity as a kingdom disciple requires nothing less than your all-out dedication toward its end goal.

God will not open the Bible for you, push you down to your knees, and blow a bugle horn when He has something to tell you. He won't make you obey Him and apply spiritual truth to your life's decisions. Spiritual growth, maturity, and development is on you. How bad do *you* want it? The answer to that question will determine your rate of growth because the answer to that question will determine the rate of effort you are willing to put into it.

When employers interview potential employees, they look at the résumé, skill, and background. But a good interviewer will also seek to discern how badly the person applying wants to succeed at the job. Now, I didn't say how badly he or she wants the job. No, because the motivation for wanting the job could stop with getting the job. They will want to know how badly this person wants to succeed at the job because that will oftentimes predict effort and success.

Friend, how badly do you want to be a living, breathing, committed kingdom disciple? Only you can determine the amount of effort and commitment you are willing to put in to personal growth. No one else is going to make you grow.

Spiritual Milk Versus Spiritual Meat

Maturity happens as you move from "milk" to "meat." The reasons a baby cannot digest a steak are multiple, but the primary reasons are the baby has neither the teeth to chew nor the digestive system to fully break down the meat. A brand-new Christian needs the milk of God's Word for a season. No believer progresses from birth to maturity overnight. But anyone who has been a Christian for any length of time and who is still on milk has remained there due to their own lack of effort toward growth.

So that raises a question: what is milk and what is meat? A lot of people think that meat is the accumulation of biblical information and milk is the lack of biblical depth. But that is not the case. A person can be full of Bible knowledge and still be a baby Christian. Meat refers to the ability to transfer what has been learned into the decision-making process of life, so that the person operates from a spiritual rather than earthly perspective. If that transfer into applying the truth has not happened, then the person remains a baby Christian.

Like a hungry baby being unable to chew meat, a person hoping to learn to transfer the truth of God's Word into their daily life choices must learn how to chew through (meditating and using) the principles of Scripture. He or she must break down the Scriptures for use. Having a ton of meat on a ton of plates sitting in front of someone will do absolutely no good toward nourishing that person's life. It's only when that meat is ingested and put to use that the value of the meat comes forth. As we noted in the beginning of this chapter, however, many Christians "have come to need milk and not solid food" (Heb. 5:12).

When a believer can partake only of milk, he or she can digest the elementary principles but not "the word of righteousness" (v. 13). It's like when a student starts school, they have to begin with the basics. We call them the fundamentals. First it is the ABCs, and then phonics before actual reading and understanding can occur. A student cannot move on to books if they do not yet know the alphabet. They can't move on to algebra if they do not yet understand addition. Without the foundation, the advanced learning cannot take place.

That's why certain classes in high school and college have prerequisites. The "prerequisites," or fundamental classes, must be completed before attempting the advanced ones. This is because all teachers know that advancement in learning occurs progressively—just like discipleship and spiritual growth.

The elementary principles of God's Word are essential but they are not the end. They are to serve as a starting point of progress toward spiritual awareness and understanding with the end

> *Growth is measured by practicing the Word. If it isn't showing up in your words, and choices, then you have not grown.*

being even your very senses can "discern good and evil." And your choices reflect that discernment. As the factual truths of Scripture are the basis of our decisions, we are then living life spiritually.

But there is a huge difference between being in a class gaining cognitive understanding of the approach, and actually being in the neighborhood and at the workplace where there are questions, challenges, persecution, and opportunities to practice your faith before others.

It doesn't matter how many times you say "amen" in church if what you learn does not flesh itself out in your actual life encounters and choices. A true kingdom disciple carries the knowledge and insight of God's Word into every moment of his or her decisions and conversations. It has to show up on the field of life; only then does it become meat. Hebrews 5 tells us that as you mature in discipleship, your senses will be able to discern the right or wrong things to think, say, and do. You will begin to operate from a heavenly rather than earthly perspective.

Growth is measured by practicing the Word. If it isn't showing up in your words, thoughts, and choices, then you have not grown. You have merely observed, like a fan rather than an actual player. It is the skill of using the Word of God in every area of life that produces growth and maturity.

Spiritual maturity demands spiritual responsibility. Solid food is for the mature, for those who are serious about growth.

And the proof of this maturity is discernment. In the spiritual realm, your senses are designed for you to be able to see things from God's point of view. What discipleship does is "train" your spiritual senses on how to discern.

The Greek word used for "trained" in verse 14 is the root form for our English word "gymnasium." It is the same term that means to work out. So through discipleship, God is taking your senses to the gym in order that they may be increased in their sensitivities to what is God's point of view and what is humanity's point of view. When you can discern wisely, you can thus choose wisely.

If you place a shiny marble next to a toddler and also place a diamond next to her as well, the toddler will more often than not gravitate to the shiny marble. Why? Because the toddler's senses are not trained to yet discern between what is flashy and what is valuable. But if you put an adult next to both objects, the adult will grab the diamond because he understands the value of the item, even though it may look less flashy and less colorful to the naked eye.

Discerning life spiritually involves more than seeing things with the naked eye. When you do so, you gain the ability to discern the true value of what comes your way. You will be less likely to become tricked by the flashy, colorful temptations, hoodwinked by Satan, or duped by smooth-talking individuals. Rather, you will discern wisely who, what, where carries the most value eternally for your life.

Kingdom discipleship gives you the ability to see beyond the obvious and access God's point of view on the matter. Remember, if all you see is what you can see then you do not see all there is to be seen. Spiritual maturity provides you with the ability to see beyond the tangible into the intangible realities of the spiritual realm and truth with the result that you can experience heaven's authority in history.

Not only will you discern truth for your own life, but as a mature kingdom disciple you will also teach others. The mark of a true disciple is that this person mentors, models, guides, and helps others toward a greater level of spiritual maturity as well. As you progress, you will naturally assist others in progressing too. Thus, you will fully become a living example of Christ's commission to go, baptize, and teach others.

Does that mean you will become a full-time minister? No, not necessarily. But it does mean that as you go in your daily life, you will naturally lead others toward a deeper relationship with Christ, and a greater understanding of His Word. You will not merely be a kingdom disciple, you will become a kingdom disciple maker.

CHAPTER 8

The Heavenly Incentive

T he church where I have gratefully served as pastor for over forty years now employs over two hundred people. It's a large staff for a church, but we focus so heavily on community impact and outreach that much of our staff is dedicated to that portion of ministry. Every year we conduct what are called "performance reviews."

These performance reviews analyze how the employee worked during the previous year. This assessment counts toward many things, such as the potential of a pay increase, additional bonuses, and even whether the employee should be on probation or let go. Every employee is aware of this process and while I would hope they carry out their jobs unto the Lord and out of the pure goodness of their hearts, I'm sure that this review is in the back of their minds.

Rewards are important, and they provide us with an additional motivating factor to do excellently at all we do. The hope is that great work will bring with it a reward and benefit related to what has been done.

Friend, God may not have a formal "performance review"

that He conducts annually. But His Son tells us that He prunes the vines that produce fruit and cuts off entirely the vines that produce nothing (John 15:1–6). One look at nature and her amazing ability to produce, reproduce, and provide for her own will give you insight into God's heart and character. He is just as interested in growth, development, and production as any owner would be. "The earth is the Lord's and all it contains" (Ps. 24:1). He cares what happens to His creation and those He loves and has placed on earth.

A Return on Your Investment

Your decisions as a kingdom disciple are an investment not only in your present rewards but also in your eternal rewards. There is a return on your investment for all that you do for the King and His kingdom.

Jesus tells us this in many places in Scripture, but one particular conversation with His disciples sheds light in a very detailed manner. It is found in three of the Gospels, but we will focus on Mark's account (10:17–31). The conversation follows an encounter Christ had with a man known to us as the "rich young ruler." This successful leader confided in Christ that he had been a very good man. He had, according to him, kept all of the laws from his youth on up. But Jesus challenged him in a way that tested his dedication. Jesus told him that if he truly loved others then he should sell all he has and give to the poor. Then he could come and spend the remainder of his days as a disciple of Christ.

The rich young ruler balked at the level of commitment Jesus asked him to demonstrate. He was more attached to his material goods than his spiritual gain, so he refused and left the presence of Christ, despondent and grieving. The Bible tells us he left in this manner because he "owned much property" (v. 22).

The disciples observed all this, and it triggered a question and thought in their own minds. Peter spoke up after the man walked away. Peter said boldly, "Behold, we have left everything and followed You" (v. 28). Perhaps he wanted accolades, or just some recognition in that moment.

Peter came from a prosperous fishing business. He was making money, and enjoying friends and family. But when Jesus showed up, he folded his nets, left his company, and followed Him. Another disciple, Matthew, left his tax-collecting business. And a tax-collecting business was a profitable business on any day. But he gave it all up to follow Jesus. These disciples had made a public allegiance to Jesus Christ when Jesus Christ was not yet known for the Savior that He is. They risked it all on a man they chose to believe when few believed. If you study church history at all, you will know that not only did these disciples leave all to follow Christ but for the majority of them, it cost them all—their very lives for their public association with Christ.

Peter wanted to know what they would get out of it. After all, Jesus had just told the rich young ruler to sell all his possessions and give to the poor. Not only that, Jesus told this man he would have treasure. Treasure in heaven. So Peter wanted to know what was his treasure.

It's not a wrong question to ask. If you are a businessperson, you know that you always seek a return on your investment. If you are a student in college, you will want a good-paying job for your work and for the cost of your degree. When you buy something at the store, you pay a price but expect a reward—the item you bought. Peter and the other disciples had paid a cost. Now they simply wanted to know what was the reward of being a kingdom disciple.

Jesus answered Peter directly. He didn't give him a parable. He didn't change the subject. He didn't rebuke him for a lack of faith. No, on this occasion, Jesus responded to the hearts of those who had left all to follow Him, and He responded clearly. He said,

> Truly I say to you, there is no one who has left house or brothers or sisters or mother or father or children or farms, for My sake and for the gospel's sake, but that he will receive a hundred times as much now in the present age, houses and brothers and sisters and mothers and children and farms, along with persecutions; and in the age to come, eternal life. But many who are first will be last, and the last, first. (vv. 29–31)

This is one of the occasions when Jesus speaks directly on the subject of rewards. He not only heard the words of Peter, but He felt the hearts of all the disciples who probably sat there wondering if their sacrificial decision had been so wise after all. It's easy to jump out and commit to something based on emotion. Many people have done that. But now the disciples were knee-deep in sacrifice, uncertainty, rejection, ridicule, and loss of the comforts of family and friends. Jesus assured them that He understood the price they paid for their public association with Him cost them something. And He assured them that this cost would be repaid at a greater level than they had ever imagined.

Matthew and Luke also report this conversation. In Luke, it is written that Jesus specifically referred to those who left all "for the kingdom of God" (Luke 18:28–30). These were truly kingdom disciples who had not compromised God's rule over every area of their lives. As a reminder, a kingdom disciple is a person who takes part in progressively learning to bring his or her entire life under the lordship of Jesus Christ. And when you live as a kingdom disciple, Jesus says there is a reward you can expect to receive. Jesus says that reward is even a hundred times as much as what you sacrificed. What's more is that Jesus also says to the things you give up—houses, farms, families—are the things you will get back—plus eternal life.

The irony is the very thing you felt you lost by becoming a disciple of Christ is not only preserved, but it is actually multiplied in return. What throws most people, though, is the uncertainty of when that return on investment will come. If you and I knew that after three months we would receive our reward, we would probably happily sacrifice. But in the spiritual realm, your reward could take months, years, decades, or even wait until eternity with Him. Because of this uncertainty of timing, too many people are not willing to pay the cost of true discipleship. Living as a disciple means living entirely by faith that the Christ you follow will make good on His Word.

> *Jesus assured them that this cost would be repaid at a greater level than they ever imagined.*

When I was younger, I caught a glimpse of God rewarding commitment to Him as a disciple. While in seminary, I worked the night shift at the Trailways bus station. It was called the dead-man shift because it lasted all night long. After a few weeks on the job, I was approached about a scheme the employees had going on. Someone would punch you in even though you weren't in, and you could sleep an hour longer than your normal break allowed. With this plan in place, people were getting paid when they were not working. In fact, they were getting paid when they were sleeping. It was wrong. I knew it was wrong, and I knew I would not take part in it at all.

So when I was approached about taking my turn of punching someone else in and out, I declined. I told them as a follower of Jesus Christ, I could not do what they were asking me to do.

Their response was straightforward enough: "You don't have a choice, Evans. Everyone does it."

To which I politely told them I could not. Due to my faith, I would not partake in their scam. As you might imagine, the rest of the employees didn't like that and began to "persecute" me for not participating. Remember, in Jesus's words to the disciples, He said the rewards do come with "persecution." Which is exactly what I faced. When five of us were supposed to be unloading a bus, the other four would sit down and watch me do it by myself. And after they had watched me, they left me, and I felt isolated. Scenarios like that played out for an entire month simply because I wouldn't go along with their deception.

One evening around three months into the scam I got a call to come to the front office where I was told that they had a suspicion about what was going on during the night shift. They had sent one of the supervisors to go around at night and check it out.

The supervisor noticed that most everyone was taking part in the scam but that I wasn't. As a result, he promoted me over everyone else and made me the night supervisor.

Unbeknownst to me, God had been preparing me for this reward that would help our family financially while I was in seminary. The Lord rewarded my public commitment to Him. The results of my persecution were experienced not only in the here and now, but I know they will also be in eternity. God rewards your commitment to Him as well. That's one of the greatest benefits of being a kingdom disciple. The reward may not come immediately, but it will come.

> *God rewards your commitment to Him as well. The reward may not come immediately, but it will come.*

What Jesus was telling His disciples in the conversation we have looked at in this chapter is that, "Yes, there is going to be loss, inconvenience, and even persecution if you are publicly associated with Me and My values. But I want to let you know that no one will lose anything as a result of being My disciple who will not gain it back at some point in the future, at an even higher level than what was lost." Friend, there are rewards for discipleship. They may not be immediate but they are enormous. What's more: they will be public.

SAVING FOR ETERNITY

Just as Jesus Christ demands a public association with Him when you are a disciple, He will also publicly reward you in eternity. Let's take a look at this in His parable found in Luke 19:11–26. A nobleman gave ten of his slaves the same amount of money to conduct business on his behalf while he was away "to receive a kingdom for himself" (v. 12). When the master "returned, after receiving the kingdom, he ordered that these slaves, to whom he had given the money, be called to him in order that he might know what business they had done."

In Jesus' parable, the nobleman's return refers to Christ's second coming, when He will call His people to account for how they served Him as a kingdom disciple. Then the issue will be, "How did My kingdom benefit by what I provided to you?"

Now, a lot of us will be able to show how God's gifts benefited us. But that's not the question. The issue with a disciple is, how did the King's business fare under your management? Is the King better off? Was His agenda furthered?

The Bible calls this day of evaluation for kingdom disciples "the judgment seat of Christ." It is described in two key passages. The first of these important passages is in 1 Corinthians 3. I want to quote it in its entirety because it is so crucial:

> According to the grace of God which was given to me, like a wise master builder I laid a foundation, and another is building on it. But each man must be careful how he builds on it. For no man can lay a foundation other than the one which is laid, which is Jesus Christ. Now if any man builds on the foundation with gold, silver, precious stones, wood, hay, straw, each man's work will become evident; for the day will show it because it is to be revealed with fire, and the fire itself will test the quality of each man's work. If any man's work which he has built on it remains, he will receive a reward. If any man's work is burned up, he will suffer loss; but he himself will be saved, yet so as through fire. (vv. 10–15)

We must be careful what kind of building we construct on the foundation God gives us. Expressed another way, we must be attentive to our life choices. The reason is that our devotion and works will be tested one day, and they will have to withstand the fire of Christ's judgment on "that day."

Paul's reference is to the day when Christ will judge His people—not for salvation but for rewards—based on our work as His disciples. This day is described in 2 Corinthians 5:10–11a: "For we must all appear before the judgment seat of Christ, so that each one may be recompensed for his deeds in the body, according to what he has done, whether good or bad. Therefore, knowing the fear of the Lord, we persuade men."

Hebrews 10:30 says that "The Lord will judge His people." On the day of evaluation, the fire of Jesus Christ "will test the quality of each man's work" (1 Cor. 3:13).

Do you appreciate sloppy work? Neither do I. I don't know too many mothers who are satisfied when their children do the dishes or clean their rooms in a sloppy, halfhearted way. Your boss certainly doesn't want sloppy work. It's not acceptable for an administrative assistant to say, "So what if your letter is full of errors and misspelled words? At least I typed it." No, that's not professional, nor is it acceptable.

God wants quality work from His disciples too. At His judgment seat, Jesus Christ is going to evaluate how well our time, talents, and treasures were used for Him—whether they were used to produce quality work or thrown-together junk. So the question is, Are you giving God's kingdom a quality return on the time, talents, and treasures He has blessed you with? Or is God getting your leftovers?

Paul called the judgment seat of Christ a thing that should cause us to fear, or be in awe. This will be a serious judgment. The reason is that when you are dealing with something expensive, you want it done right. If it's something just thrown together, you don't care. But if you're building an expensive house and the bricks aren't laid right, you're going to get that corrected.

Let somebody even look like he's going to ding the door of your expensive car, and you become upset. You won't even park it beside other cars where it could possibly get dinged. The more something costs, the more serious you are going to be about it.

God paid a high price for you and me. We cost Him the life of His Son. Not only that, but He has entrusted us with the stewardship of His kingdom. He has given us the privilege of ruling with Him in His kingdom.

Are we going to turn around and give God sloppy work, our leftover time, talents, and treasures? Are we going to give the school district our best teaching efforts then throw something together on Saturday night to teach the kids at Sunday school?

Are we going to spend thousands of dollars on our houses and cars and clothes and then toss a little tip toward God? No, God says all of this cost Him too much to let us get away with shoddy work ourselves. We are going to be evaluated. The Bible says whatever you get in time, talents, and treasures, make sure you give God His portion first. Because if you don't, you won't have any rewards later. You won't have any talents left over at the end of life. Be sure to take care of Jesus Christ first, so that He might have "first place in everything" (Col. 1:18). That is the mark of a kingdom disciple.

Truths from the Nobleman's Story

Let's return to the nobleman's story. The nobleman comes home from his journey, and he's ready to call his servants in to account for how they used their minas and represented his interests. The first servant came and said, "Master, your mina has made ten minas more" (Luke 19:16). That's a 1,000 percent increase! This man has obviously invested his master's money well. He could say, "Master, I took what you gave me and invested it, and I had fun doing it. Look at what I have for you."

What does the master—remember, he represents Christ in this parable—say to this man who so effectively used what he had been given for the kingdom? He receives a threefold reward. The first reward is public recognition, the master's public announcement, "Well done" (v. 17). When you show up at His judgment seat, there will be nothing like hearing Jesus say, "Well done!" He is going to say it publicly. You may be hidden away in your work, but if you do what God has called you to do faithfully and consistently, you will be honored before all of heaven on that day.

The second reward this faithful disciple received was a kingdom inheritance. The master said, "Because you have been faithful in a very little thing, you are to be in authority over ten cities" (v. 17).

Most people have a wrong view of the eternal kingdom. We will not be floating around on clouds. The eternal kingdom will be a government, which will operate in perfect righteousness. There will be people in positions of authority who were faithful servants of Jesus Christ on earth. Just as a good worker gets a promotion, so Christ's faithful disciples will get promotions in the kingdom. Some will manage ten cities.

But this faithful disciple got a third reward. It was a surprise, a bonus. You'll find it in verse 24. He got the mina that the master had originally given to the third person. When Jesus Christ comes, He is going to look at those who were not faithful and snatch away from them what little bit they did.

You may think that's not fair. But we need to remember one thing. Christ is going to make sure His kingdom resources aren't wasted. If we fail to grasp an opportunity for kingdom service, Christ will give it to someone else and we will lose out.

The second disciple also had a good report, although he wasn't as productive as the first. "Your mina, master, has made five minas." So the master told him, "You are to be over five cities" (vv. 18–19).

Did you notice that this disciple didn't get any public recognition? He got his five cities, but no "Well done." I believe the reason is that he was only half-faithful.

Then there's the third individual. I won't refer to him as a disciple because his actions did not reveal that. He brought his mina and said, "Master, here is your mina, which I kept put away in a handkerchief; for I was afraid of you, because you are an exacting man" (vv. 20–21).

In effect, this man was saying, "Master, I just want you to know I didn't lose your money. I kept it safe and sound under my mattress. I took the time, talents, and treasures you gave me and stored them away, because you are a hard master."

This guy had been playing both ends against the middle. Here was his reasoning: "I am not going to break my neck serving my master. He is going away on some long trip. He may not even come back. He may forget all about me.

"In the meantime, I've got my own business to tend to. I've got my own house to build and money to make and talents to use. But just in case he does come back, I'll make sure I don't lose what he gave me. I'll play it safe and hide his mina."

The master told this person, "By your own words I will judge you, you worthless slave" (v. 22). Then he asked him, "Why did you not put my money in the bank, and having come, I would have collected it with interest?" (v. 23). He couldn't even give this person an E for effort, and he was called wicked because he knew putting the money in the bank meant that there would be a record.

I'm afraid there are many Christians who can talk about the grace and goodness of God, who can praise Him for taking them from nowhere to somewhere, but who are not giving Him a decent return on His investment in them.

These people are not only failing to return 1,000 or 500 or even 10 percent to God. Like the faithless follower, they aren't even producing the 2 or 3 percent they could get down at the local bank. The master says that people like that are no good to him.

> *Many Christians who talk about the goodness of God are not giving Him a decent return on His investment in them.*

So in contrast to the first disciple, this person receives a ringing condemnation. He gets no cities, and as we saw above, even the mina he has is taken away from him. He gets the same amount of credit as profit he produced for the master: none.

Notice the involvement of the "bystanders" (v. 24) in this man's judgment. I don't know how God is going to do it, but somehow the results of Christ's judgment seat will be visible to everyone. Maybe God will use a cosmic video screen. Whatever the method, others will know the results.

That means if we are simply wearing the name of Christ like

a decoration instead of living it, everyone will know. If we have nothing to bring to Christ that can withstand the fire, other believers at His judgment seat will know.

That's why I think there will be some big surprises on that day, with people saying, "But I thought so-and-so was a good Christian. He always came to church with his Bible under his arm. He was always saying 'Praise the Lord.'" But if there is no depth to the commitment carried out in personal sacrifice, investment, and service, it will become obvious on that day.

This is enough to scare me. This is enough to shake me up. I don't want my life to be put on public display and find out I came in third like the worthless servant. I don't want to see my work snatched from me. I want to be a faithful servant who makes the most of what his Master has entrusted to him.

I don't want to be just a professional Christian but an authentic kingdom disciple. I know you do too, influencing many to enter the kingdom of God. So in part 3, we will apply the principles of kingdom discipleship to the four spheres of the kingdom: the individual, family, church, and community.

The Function of Kingdom Discipleship

CHAPTER 9

The Individual

Unlike the elegant *Titanic* described in chapter 1, filled with wealthy voyagers, the *Pelicano* was once the most unwanted ship in the world. For over two years it floated on the open seas. It could be called the *Flying Dutchman* of the twentieth century. No port would accept it.

The massive ship was turned away from at least eleven countries, including Honduras, Costa Rica, Guinea-Bissau, the Bahamas, and the island country of Cape Verde. It wandered the Caribbean, went to West Africa, sailed the Mediterranean, and roamed the Indian Ocean. It was only allowed to dock long enough to refuel and then go back to sea again.

During those years, the orphan ship had even undergone name changes before it became the *Pelicano*. It actually left America as the *Khian Sea*, was renamed the *Felicia* two years later, and became the ill-fated *Pelicano* four months after that.

The reason for the wide-scale rejection of the *Pelicano* is because in 1986 the City of Brotherly Love, Philadelphia, didn't have much brotherly love at all. The sanitation workers said they didn't feel that love from the city that managed them. So they went on strike for almost an entire month.

A lot of trash can accumulate in a month in a city the size of Philadelphia. At first they tried to ship their trash to Ohio and Georgia. But the states refused to accept it. What Philadelphia ended up doing was incinerating their trash into 28 million pounds of scrap and ash, and dumping it into the belly of a ship later called the *Pelicano*.

The *Pelicano* became an infamous floating garbage dump with megatons of rotting trash containing toxic elements from arsenic to lead. No nation around the entire world wanted the *Pelicano* anywhere near them. It had a cargo of trash that it couldn't get rid of.

The Toxic Trash of Our Lives

Life has a way of unloading its junk on us, too, sometimes. Due to our sins, circumstances, and also because of things others have done to us, either intentionally or unintentionally, we get burdened under the weight of trash.

In fact, over time this trash becomes downright toxic. It produces the fumes of anger, guilt, pessimism, fear, and bitterness. Contamination grows out of the stagnation and rots us away. Even other people can smell our stench when we come around.

So we end up floating from one person to another person, or from one situation to another situation, only to discover that we get to hang around long enough to get some fuel, but no longer than that. No one wants our trash.

Even we don't want our trash. So we go to counselors to try and get rid of it. But we notice that when we leave, we still have it with us. So then we go to church to get rid of it, and we feel good for a moment, but a few sniffs after the service and we discover that we still have our trash. There doesn't seem to be anyplace that can free us from the burden of our trash.

If you can identify with the *Pelicano* today, then you know what it is like to feel aimless and weary under a heavy burden. Weary is different than sleepy. You can fix sleepy with a bed, or with a nap in the easy chair.

But weary dictates to you how you will feel and what you will do. Weary means you can no longer relax. Weary means you are no longer able to be at home with who you are. You have lost your joy. You need relief even from yourself because the thirty-million-pound toxic ash heap that has piled up within you prevents you from having peace.

If "weary" describes you, then I have good news for you. Living as a kingdom disciple has a way of unloading some weight from your shoulders. Jesus says that He offers victory for kingdom disciples from what weighs you down. Jesus doesn't want to be just living in you but to rule in your life so that you are an overcomer (Rom. 5:17; John 16:33; 1 John 5:4–5; Rev. 12:11). Experiencing His ruling authority is intimately tied to your relationship with Him. This victory comes through one of the greatest words in the Scripture: "Rest."

Jesus says that He has come to give you rest. Would you like some rest? Would you like some peace? As you grow in your maturity as a kingdom disciple (a man or woman who is progressively living all of life under the lordship of Jesus Christ), you will discover that Jesus offers you what no one else ever could. He gives you a place to dock. He gives you a way to be rid of your burdens. He gives you not only a rest in heaven but also an ongoing rest while on earth. But before He does, He gives three instructions: come, take, and learn.

REST IS FOR DEPENDENT PEOPLE ONLY

Jesus once prayed, "I praise You, Father, Lord of heaven and earth, that You have hidden these things from the wise and intelligent and have revealed them to infants" (Matt. 11:25). This statement prefaced His invitation to rest in v. 28: "Come to Me all who are weary and heavy-laden." Why say "You have . . . revealed these things to infants"? Because God does not reveal Himself to the proud and the self-sufficient, but only to the humble.

Anyone who thinks he is smart enough to fix his own life isn't ready to admit his need and draw close to God. But infants are helpless and totally dependent on their parents. Infants can't do anything themselves. All they can do is cry out in need and wait for someone to help them.

Now, I wasn't raised with money. I was raised in row houses in an urban community in Baltimore where my parents just barely made it. Sometimes my mom would have to find a way to cook the fish my dad caught for breakfast, lunch, dinner, and dessert. But despite this reality, I never went to bed worried. The load of life didn't dawn on me very much at all. The reason I never struggled with life as a young child was because it wasn't my problem. That was my parents' problem. I let them worry about it.

When my dad would be laid off for weeks on end due to no work as a longshoreman, I didn't stress. I relied on those who were responsible to care for us. See, dependency does have its benefits—like peace, rest, contentment.

As an adult, I understand the weight of life's burdens. I experienced it myself, especially as a young man with four small children, a wife, and the challenge of balancing full-time academia with providing for my family. Yet despite all we carry on us as we become adults, Jesus says that if you and I will simply grow in the fundamental principles of discipleship, we can rest. We can experience one of the greatest benefits of being His: peace.

The answers to life's burdens are not found in your knowledge, success, or even in "human wisdom" as Jesus mentioned in the verse we just looked at. In fact, not only can you not find the ways to victory on your own, it is actually hidden from you. Speaking to God concerning spiritual truth, Jesus said, "You have hidden these things from the wise and intelligent." Those who believe they are so smart in human understanding don't get the divine viewpoint. Only true kingdom disciples access the wisdom of the Father—wisdom that can radically transform our lives and give us all we need to live both abundantly and victoriously and with kingdom authority.

JESUS OFFERS REST: "COME TO ME"

To those who recognize their need for God and commit to living as kingdom disciples, Jesus offers this invitation:

> Come to Me, all who are weary and heavy-laden, and I will give you rest. Take My yoke upon you and learn from Me, for I am gentle and humble in heart, and you will find rest for your souls. For My yoke is easy and My burden is light. (Matt. 11:28–30)

Talk about rest and relief from burdens. "Heavy-laden" means the weight is simply too heavy to bear. It's like a weightlifter with all those disks on both sides of the bar, struggling to hold the barbell up. Similarly, the burdens of life may be weighing you down. Those afflictions may include physical pain, mistakes, regrets, demands, and disappointments. Eventually we can reach the point where we can't lift the weight anymore. We can't go on. That's why we must live as a kingdom disciple, because that is the only way to tap in to the power that can overcome all of life's challenges. When you abide in Christ and connect to Him fully, you discover His yoke is easy and His burden is light.

Yet although this gift is free, it isn't automatic. Jesus tells us that we must do three things. In His invitation, He gives us three active verbs.

The first active verb is "Come." To come to Him, you must leave your human wisdom and attempts at self-sufficiency behind. It's like when you get sick and you run down to the corner drugstore to try and fix it yourself, but nothing seems to work. That's when you realize that you need to go and see a doctor. You visit the doctor because he has information that is beyond your scope of knowledge. He has equipment that is beyond your ability to diagnose and an investigative process to analyze the data in order to identify the source of your ailment. He has training, history, understanding, and expertise that extends beyond you.

God will let you do everything that you want to do in using all of your human ingenuity to seek to live victoriously. He will let you try, and fail, so that you will discover that the only way to live as a victorious kingdom disciple is through Him. That is where you will find rest.

"Rest" is a big word in the Bible, going all the way back to the beginning of Scripture. We read that God worked for six days but on the seventh day, He rested (Gen. 2:2–3). He didn't take a nap. That's not what rest meant. What it meant is that God "chilled." He sat back and enjoyed His creation. So important was this rest that God told Israel to honor the Sabbath as a day of rest. He prohibited them from working so that there would be a season when they could reflect on all God had done for them, and was doing.

See, rest reminds us of our dependence on God. It reminds us of the core principle of abiding in Christ. When we begin to falsely believe that our results are because of us, we lose focus on what a truly abundant life springs from. In fact, God is so able to provide for you in spite of you that it says, "It is vain for you to rise up early, to retire late, to eat the bread of painful labors; for He gives to His beloved *even in his sleep*" (Ps. 127:2, emphasis added). God is still working on stuff while you are snoring. Rest means to put the processes and outcomes ultimately in the hands of God, where they belong. Another word for rest is surrender. But since there are so many internal resistances to the word "surrender," let's continue focusing on this concept of rest—the ability to let go and let God.

> *Rest reminds us of our dependence on God and the core principle of abiding in Christ.*

Thursday is the day when the garbage pickup service comes down our street. And despite more than three decades of living in the same home, I have never had the pickup person come to my door and ask where my trash is. If I didn't take the trash to the curb, I'm going to have to live with it for another week. So I take the trash to the curb because the stench from the rottenness would consume our entire home.

When He died on the cross, Jesus signed us all up for the

ability to receive trash pickup service. But we still need to come. He will not force His rest on you. He says, "Come to Me" because in order to come to Him, you must leave behind the worldly wisdom within your own four walls. Jesus says, "Come to Me," and when you do, bring your trash with you. But not only do you bring your burdens to the Lord, you also hand off the pressure that comes from living in a sinful environment.

You might be saying, "Tony, what is our trash anyhow?" Our trash is anything contrary to the truth of God that holds you back from completely living out your personal destiny. It includes those fortresses that have been erected in your mind. "For as he thinks within himself, so he is" (Prov. 23:7). Every wrong attitude, thought, or belief results in wrong behavior, strongholds, addictions, or bondage.

GIVE HIM YOUR BURDENS

In football, once the quarterback receives the ball from the center, he's under a lot of pressure. Players from the other team are trying to tear at him or sack him. But if the quarterback turns and hands the ball to the halfback or running back, the pressure that was once on him now goes to the other player. The quarterback can literally stand there and watch the rest of the play once he hands the ball off. No one will touch him.

Similarly, when you are trying to live your life by your own effort, strength, and wisdom, you get to experience the pressure of the world's attacks and circumstances upon you. Jesus says if you will hand off the ball of burdens to Him as a kingdom disciple abiding in Him—yoked to Him—He will carry it all. You can rest.

I was talking once with a couple that was engaged. They

wanted to marry, but there was a problem they had asked me to help resolve. The woman had accumulated a considerable amount of debt over the years, and the couple just couldn't see getting married with all of this debt. So after explaining the situation to me, I turned to the husband and said, "We can resolve this fairly easily."

He looked surprised and then asked me how. I told him, "If you simply turn to her and tell her that her debt is no longer her debt—that you'll take it—then there is your solution."

His response was quiet, pondering what I had said, so I continued. "Do you love her?" I asked.

"Yes, of course," he replied.

"Do you want to marry her?" I also asked.

"Absolutely," he replied.

"Then let her know that it's no longer her burden to bear. Let her know it's yours."

After thinking about it for the rest of the day, this man agreed to do that. They called me back to tell me and I could "hear" the tears in the voice of the lady as she shared her relief. See, she had a load, but she also had a love. And when the love was willing to take the load, she found rest. Jesus will take your load—no matter if you were the one who created the mess. He'll take it when you make Him your central point in all of life and abide in Him.

Fundamentally, this verse is an invitation to salvation. Coming to Him means bringing your sin while seeking His grace and forgiveness. This solidifies an eternal rest: salvation. "I will give you rest." But He also invites you to abide in an ongoing rest and victory: sanctification. He does this by moving to our second verb, "Take." He says, "Take My yoke upon you."

Harnessed Together: "Take My Yoke"

Jesus' instructions may raise a question. How can He talk about yokes and loads, which suggest hard work, and about rest in the same breath? To most of us, rest means kicking back in the recliner. But that's not the kind of rest Jesus is offering.

A yoke is a harness that goes around the necks of two oxen so they can pull a load. Accepting Jesus' yoke is a picture of surrender to Him, but it's also a picture of help because you're not pulling the load alone. Jesus is yoked with you, and He's going to take the lead and the load.

The purpose of yoking two oxen together was threefold. First, it created companionship because they were hooked side by side. Second, it taught surrender, because in the agricultural days of the Bible, an older, stronger ox was most always hooked up with a younger ox; thus the younger ox learned how to surrender and do the job correctly. The younger ox had to submit to the experience, size, and strength of the older one. This allowed the younger ox to lean on the power and authority of the older one. Third, there was shared responsibility because each is pulling the same plow. The younger ox was able to fulfill its purpose through the wisdom and power of the older ox. Like a car hitched to a tow truck, a person yoked with Christ can go farther than they ever could on their own because you are sharing in His kingdom authority.

My son Jonathan travels with me a lot when I speak. On one occasion, he was with me and I had requested that we both upgrade to first class based on my Platinum Flyer award miles. With platinum status, I'm able to upgrade a companion to first class as well. But on this particular trip, I got upgraded while Jonathan remained in coach.

We went to the front desk to ask why Jonathan wasn't upgraded, especially since he's not only a companion but also my son. We were told they were not able to upgrade him because he had purchased his ticket apart from mine. His indicator number was different from mine, so he was unable to enjoy the benefits that come from being linked with me on that flight.

Many of us as God's children can't fully enjoy the benefits of living yoked with Christ because we have our own indicator numbers. We belong to God, sure, but we insist on plowing our own fields, going our own way, and following our own will. We wonder why no power is evident in our lives and the reason is simple. You don't get the companion benefits of Christ if you don't yoke with Him as a companion. To take His yoke upon you means you willingly choose to go where He says to go, do what He says to do, think what He says to think. You choose to surrender. Your victory as a kingdom disciple is entirely related to your level of surrender.

> *To take His yoke upon you means you willingly choose to go where He says to go. You choose to surrender.*

To fully enjoy relief from your burdens, you have to bow your head and be willing to accept His yoke. You must abide in a relationship with Him and His Word, as we have seen earlier. It is more than just accumulating information about Him.

It involves staying connected to Him. He wants you to make your companionship with Him not only the most important thing, but an ongoing and continual relationship. An ox doesn't yoke and take a few steps only to then unyoke and take a few more. To yoke with someone is to agree to walk with them where and how they are leading.

Jesus promises that because He is gentle and humble, His yoke is easy. The Greek word for easy is the word "well-fitted," or you could also say "custom made." His yoke has been designed with you in mind.

It won't be wearisome or confining or constricting to you. It will be liberating.

"LEARN FROM ME"

We've pulled up to the dock of Jesus Christ in response to His instruction to "Come." We've joined Him through tying up with Him under the connection of His yoke. Now, let's see how we can fully maximize our individual lives as His disciples through the next section of the verse.

Only the truth sets you free. To take out the trash and unload the boat is to exchange your thoughts with Christ's thoughts on a matter. Remember, our trash is anything that is contrary to the truth of God. A kingdom disciple understands the necessity of taking every thought captive unto Christ. When a thought, attitude, or impulse toward a behavior comes into your mind, you are to take it captive and align it with God's viewpoint. Because when you align your thoughts with His thoughts, then you are living as a kingdom disciple. Your thoughts affect your actions.

Thus, the third active verb Jesus gives us as an instruction is "Learn." He says, "Learn from Me, for I am gentle and humble in heart." The Greek word that we translate into "learn" is the concept of discipleship. Jesus disciples you when you learn from Him. It is done through an ongoing renewal of your mind to learn to think like His. This process doesn't happen instantaneously. It happens one thought at a time.

How do you unload thirty million pounds of toxic ash off a ship like the *Pelicano*? One pound at a time. Each time you take a thought captive and replace human wisdom with spiritual truth and insight, you are removing the burden and lessening the cargo of self-will. You are becoming more and more a kingdom disciple.

What are you supposed to be learning? Learn how Jesus pulls the plow. Learn how Jesus relates to His Father. Learn how Jesus views sin. Learn how Jesus values others. Learn what Christ's viewpoint is on a matter.

But don't only learn it; accept it—submit to it—and let it come forth in your actions. Learning from Jesus means to replace human wisdom with spiritual manifestation. It means to learn, accept, and apply His approach to peace, conquering worry, your value, your identity, what it means to be a kingdom man or a kingdom woman, overcoming temptation, operating in the workplace. It means showing respect, giving and receiving grace, learning to trust, properly handling your money. All of that, and more.

Jesus said learn My way of doing things. You tried your way and it just made you weary. Learn My way because My yoke is easy, and My burden is light. It's a new way. A new mind. It's a new yoke. God wants you to put away the old yoke that enslaved you, and exchange it for His yoke that will set you free.

FINDING REST FOR YOUR SOUL

To finish this formula for living as a kingdom disciple, let's look at the last two verses in this section in their entirety. Jesus says,

"Take My yoke upon you and learn from Me, for I am gentle and humble in heart, and you will find rest for your souls. For My yoke is easy and My burden is light."

I don't want you to misread that. Jesus never said you won't have a burden. He just said it won't weigh the same. The burden will now be light.

One day I was walking through the airport with suitcases in both hands. Someone stopped me and asked, "Don't those have wheels?" Here I was straining and struggling, all because I had forgotten that my suitcases had wheels. I quickly put both of them down, pulled the handles up, and went on my way. Now, the weight I was carrying didn't change. They were still the same full suitcases. But since I changed the way I was moving them, my burden became light. I didn't feel it as I used to.

God is saying that if you will come to Christ as a fully committed kingdom disciple, He can put wheels on your life so the circumstances and challenges you face won't weigh you down as they used to.

Our world has many problems today and they come in all shapes and sizes. Rest, peace, and joy are increasingly harder to come by. But when you yoke up with Christ, God says you will rest well.

One day two men entered into a competition as foresters to discover who could cut down the most trees in a day. The younger man's strategy was to use his size and strength. But the older man had a different strategy: every hour he would sit down and take a rest.

The younger man noticed what he was doing and mockingly laughed at him. *He can't even make an hour*, he thought. *I've got this in the bag.*

So while the younger man kept chopping and chopping and chopping, the older man would chop for fifty minutes then rest for ten, chop for fifty and then rest for ten. This went on all day long.

At the end of the day, the judge counted the trees. To everyone's surprise, the older man had chopped down twice as many trees as the younger. Everyone was confused, especially since the older man worked considerably less than the other.

When the younger man asked how he won, the old guy pointed out that he was using that downtime to sharpen his ax. See, when you've got the right thing working for you, you can take a rest. You can relax because God's got it. He can accomplish more in a minute than we ever could in a lifetime. Wouldn't it be wise to rest in His sovereign rule, yoked to Jesus Christ?

As a kingdom disciple, remember this one phrase: God's got it. Rest in Him through pursuing an intimate relationship with Christ, and He will do more in you and through you than you could have ever done on your own as He shares His kingdom authority with you.

CHAPTER 10

The Family

Even before there was sin, there was the concept of family. God had a great plan for man and woman and the first family on earth. Placed in a sinless environment created by God, Adam and Eve had everything they needed, and God gave them authority over all His creation. God blessed them. In Genesis 1 we read,

> God said, "Let Us make man in Our image according to Our likeness; and let them rule over the fish of the sea and over the birds of the sky and over the cattle and over all the earth, and over every creeping thing that creeps on the earth." God created man in His own image, in the image of God He created him; male and female He created them. God blessed them; and God said to them, "Be fruitful and multiply, and fill the earth, and subdue it; and rule over the fish of the sea and over the birds of the sky and over every living thing that moves on the earth." (vv. 26–28)

God gave mankind the commission to bear the Trinitarian image of God—"Us" refers to the triune God (Father, Son, and Spirit)—as He created humanity (body, soul, and spirit) to mirror Him. Then He established them in the divine institution called family (father, mother, child) to reproduce His image.

Therefore, the goal of people in general, and the family in particular, is to mirror God in the visible realm predicated on His reality in the invisible. The family is to be the visible photograph and representation of God Himself. And so God blessed Adam and Eve with love, telling them to "be fruitful . . . and fill the earth, and subdue it." He blessed them with children (Gen. 1:28; 4:1–2). Sin by the first couple and the first family (Gen. 3:1–13, 16–19; 4:1–12) would alienate mankind until a Redeemer would rescue them from the grip of sin and Satan, the tempter.

THE KINGDOM FAMILY

A kingdom disciple is one who surrenders every area of life to the lordship of Jesus Christ. Today a kingdom family does the same. Thanks to the coming Redeemer promised in Genesis 3:15 and the Holy Spirit whom Jesus would send after His ascension, spouses and families can model the kingdom on earth. As families surrender their lives to Christ—jointly in their husband/wife and parent/child relationships toward each other and in their choices as individuals within the family unit—they can operate under divine authority, bringing honor to God.

Simply put, the family's mission is to replicate the image of God by reflecting His Son, Jesus Christ, in history and carrying out God the Father's divinely mandated dominion to "let them rule" (Gen. 1:26). Personal and familial happiness is to be a benefit of a strong family, but it's not the mission. The mission is the reflection and representation of God through the advancement of His kingdom and rule on earth. Happiness becomes the natural benefit when this goal is being realized.

The problem today is that we have transposed the benefit with the goal, so when the benefit—happiness—is not working out we quit and move on. Remember, happiness is never God's first concern. Rather, happiness and satisfaction are to be a natural outgrowth of fulfilling God's first concern: advancing His kingdom. When we make His first concern our first concern, we will experience the benefits. But if we focus on the benefit of happiness without getting back to the purpose, we may wind up losing both the purpose and the benefit.

Family was established to be God's foundational representative institution in society and provides the framework to collectively carry out the plan of God in history. In particular, that plan includes the replication of God's image through Jesus Christ and the implementation of His rule, or *dominion*, on earth. *Dominion* simply means ruling on God's behalf in history so that history comes under God's authority. And it would be through the establishment and replication of the family that would serve as the foundation for the advancement of God's kingdom rule in society.

THE DOMINION OF THE FAMILY

In review, the *dominion covenant,* first stated in Genesis 1:26, means God is delegating to mankind the full responsibility for managing His earthly creation. In letting mankind exercise direct dominion, He has placed an agent on earth to serve as His representative to carry out His desires in history.

God, who grants us the authority to rule, also grants the freedom and responsibility to rule on His behalf as owner. But what He does not do is *force* us to rule. He says, "Let them rule." He does not say He is going to make us rule.

What that means is that you can have a happy family or a miserable family depending on whether or not you are exercising your rule in reflection of God's image. God isn't going to make you rule. He isn't going to make you have a productive and fulfilling home. He sets up the fundamentals of the family, and gives you the option of utilizing them.

> *God grants us the freedom to rule. But He does not force us to rule.*

Often the well-being of the home is determined by whether the husband is reflecting Christ in his role, or the wife is reflecting Christ in hers. Once that mirror gets broken, the reflection that is supposed to happen in the relationship gets broken with it. Virtually every time there is a family breakdown, it is because one or both parties are functioning outside of the covenantal bonds of marriage. (For more on marriage as a covenant, see the section "God's Description of Marriage.") They are failing to actualize the rulership God has given to them.

Satan tries to subvert our God-given authority by having us either (1) relinquish our rule by handing it over to him through deceiving us into believing he has authority, or (2) rule poorly based on our own judgments and distorted worldviews. It isn't until we rule with surrender to the comprehensive rule of God that we will become the rulers he intended. It is then that we enter into the complete realization of the divine design for a family under God.

The Lord God: Master and Ruler

In Genesis 2 the narrative moves from the general creation to the specific creation of humanity, beginning with Adam. We read, "The LORD God formed man of dust from the ground, and breathed into his nostrils the breath of life; and man became a living being" (v. 7).

Why is this important? Because the word LORD (in small caps) references the covenant name of God, which is *Yahweh*. *Yahweh* literally translates into "master, and absolute ruler." When God introduces Himself to Adam relationally in the garden, and when He introduces Himself to us relationally through Scripture, He uses the term "LORD God." In all other references in these chapters that are not linked with man, God refers to Himself as *Elohim*, meaning Creator.

Clearly God is establishing the absolute and authoritative nature of His relationship with mankind through the revelation of His character and name. In fact, we know this is His objective because it is the first thing that Satan sought to undo when speaking with Eve later on in chapter 3 of Genesis.

It's significant that Satan did not refer to God as Yahweh (LORD God). He removed the name "LORD" and said, "Indeed, has God said . . . ?" (Gen. 3:1). Satan sought to strip God of His relationship with man as absolute ruler and authority by ignoring His name that connoted His relational position. As a result, Satan kept the idea of religion (God) while eliminating the order of authority (under God).

Religion without God as absolute ruler and authority is no threat to Satan. Life with the idea of God is much different than life under God. Life under God is kingdom discipleship. Life that seeks its own decisions and will apart from God is religion. In fact, Satan often uses organized religion to keep people from the one, true God. Ritual that is not predicated on an authoritative nature of relationship between God and mankind is simply legalism and is the fastest track away from God's purposes of dominion than any other (see Eve's deception in Genesis 3).

Before any family was established, authority was established. Authority is the key component to living as a kingdom disciple and experiencing the manifold abundance Christ came to offer you. In fact, in the very midst of forming the foundation of the family, God reinforced that foundation as being under His own rightful authority. The primary element that everything else rests upon in a kingdom is the authority of the ruler. Without the proper establishment of and adherence to a ruler, anarchy ensues.

THE FOUNDATION OF AUTHORITY BEGINS BEFORE WE MARRY

Before the concept of family ever got introduced, Adam was single. Before any family comes together and is created on earth through a marriage, both individuals are single. One of the areas we often fail to focus on in building strong families is in building strong singles. A strong single will contribute to a strong family.

You may be reading this as a single (or single-again) person. This can be the time to let God prepare you for marriage. Before we ever get family right, we need to get singlehood right. A kingdom single is an unmarried person who undistractedly prioritizes their divine calling for the advancement of God's kingdom. What an opportunity!

The name *Adam* refers to that "which comes from the ground."

God made man from the very ground that he came from and the very ground he was appointed to oversee—the place where his managerial responsibilities were to be carried out.

In order for Adam to live as a successful single, his dual frame of reference was to recognize that (1) the very ground from which he was created he was appointed to oversee and (2) he needed humility to live life under the leadership of the LORD God. As long as he kept that mindset and functioned according to that truth, he would have the tools to make productive decisions.

What Adam needed to learn before God merged him into a family was that he was to be an overseer. God gave him a job (Gen. 2:15). Adam's job also offers some wisdom for single women. Women, when you consider a man for marriage, remember that before God gave Adam a wife, God gave him responsibility. It's clear from these events that God wants a man—and husband—to work and to be responsible. That shows us that an irresponsible man, no matter how attractive or how smooth he can talk, is not a good choice for marriage. Marriage won't make him a responsible provider and leader. God wants the best for each of His daughters. Consider your choice of a mate carefully, and follow God's standard by marrying only a man who demonstrates while he is single that he can and will take care of you in marriage.

In addition to his responsibility, though, God also gave him

> *God gave man responsibility. That shows that an irresponsible man is not a good choice for marriage.*

freedom. Adam could enjoy all the fruit of the garden, with one exception: the fruit of the tree of the knowledge of good and evil (vv. 16–17). The second lesson, based on verses 16 and 17, indicates why so many marriages and families dissolve. God gave Adam work to do in the garden, and with those instructions He prepared Adam to live there. God gave only one limitation: "From the tree of the knowledge of good and evil you shall not eat, for in the day that you eat from it you will surely die" (Gen. 2:17). That conversation with Adam points us to the weakness in most homes: most husbands don't know what God has said—or they alter what God has said when applying it to their own lives and relationships.

Here is the second lesson for single men and women: if your personal foundation (humility before God and an accurate understanding and application of God's Word) is not solid before creating a new family through marriage and children, your family's foundation will not be solid either. Operating as a single kingdom disciple under the divine rule of the Lord God is the fundamental key to laying the foundation for family.

Understanding the Purpose of a Blessing

If you are already married and were not living as a kingdom disciple prior to establishing your family, or if your mate was not, then the first place to start is focusing on what it means to be a kingdom disciple. It's never too late to align your thoughts, words, and actions underneath God's overarching rule. Start with yourself, pray for your spouse, and then seek to implement discipleship principles within your home. When you do, you will receive God's abundant blessings as promised in His Word.

Pray for others in your family as well, that your children may become kingdom disciples.

Keep in mind, though, God never blesses just to bless. There is always a reason, a purpose, for His provision. Notice the order in the following verse relating to the purpose of the establishment of the family. It says: "*God blessed* them; and God said to them, 'Be fruitful and multiply, and fill the earth, and subdue it; and *rule over* the fish of the sea and over the birds of the sky and over every living thing that moves on the earth'" (Gen. 1:28, emphasis added).

First, it would help to define a blessing. A blessing is *the capacity to experience, enjoy, and extend the goodness of God in your life.* It is never just about you. While it includes you, it is also intended to extend through you to others somehow. Too many Christians today want God to bless them without being willing for God to bless others through them.

When God established the family in the garden, He told them to be fruitful and multiply. He blessed them. Then He enabled them to extend the blessing He had given them throughout the land, and to those who came after them. In addition, God also blessed them through providing them with what they needed to carry out the rule He had given to them.

A blessing is when God provides all that is needed for you to accomplish all there is under your influence in life.

Second, note that after the blessing came the instructions. God blessed, but then followed that up with the commission of Adam and Eve to be fruitful and multiply and to rule over that which He had placed under them. They were to serve as managers over the garden that had been given to them.

One of the worst things is to live your life while neglecting your garden of purpose, productivity, and divine destiny, both as individuals and as a family. The true tragedy is to miss out on managing, or even to mismanage, the sphere of responsibility God has prepared for you and your family.

GOD'S DESCRIPTION OF MARRIAGE

In Malachi 2, God complained that His people had wandered from Him. They had taken a detour from God's intended destination for them. Their wandering showed in many ways, including how they treated their marriages. God got specific:

> This is another thing you do: you cover the altar of the LORD with tears, with weeping and with groaning, because He no longer regards the offering or accepts it with favor from your hand. Yet you say, 'For what reason?' Because the LORD has been a witness between you and the wife of your youth, against whom you have dealt treacherously, though she is your companion and your wife by covenant. (vv. 13–14)

Notice the final word. God specifically describes the marriage union as a "covenant." The term "covenant" used to be regularly attached to the concept of marriage, which is the foundation for family. In fact, a kingdom marriage is defined as a covenantal union between a man and a woman who commit themselves to functioning in unity under divine authority in order to replicate God's image and expand His rule in the world through both their individual and joint callings. This union is to be the foundation for building kingdom families. However, the word has been forgotten by Christians in our contemporary language today, even though it is the biblical description of marriage used throughout Scripture.

The problems in our homes come when we don't recognize that marriage *is* a covenant. Among those who do, many simply don't know what a covenant entails. When we do not know what a covenant is, then we do not know what we are supposed to have, develop, or protect over time. It's like trying to hit a bull's-eye without a target.

A covenant is more than a formal contractual arrangement. Biblically, *a covenant is a spiritual and relational bond between God and a person, or people, inclusive of certain agreements, conditions, benefits, and effects.*

Whenever God wanted to formalize His relationship with His people, He established a covenant. There are a number of these agreements in Scripture such as the Abrahamic covenant, the Mosaic covenant, the Davidic covenant, and the new covenant. As we saw in an earlier chapter, these are formal arrangements that are spiritually binding in a legal capacity between God and a person, or people. It is through covenants that God administers His kingdom programs.

Marriage is another covenant that God has established. As such, the marriage covenant can never operate to its fullest potential without the ongoing involvement of God. Biblical, spiritual, and theological covenants assume God's integration into every aspect of the relationship in order for that covenant to maximize its purpose.

When the practical realities of God are dismissed from the marital covenantal relationship, it becomes an invitation to the devil to create havoc in the home. This happens because there has been a departure from God's overarching transcendence.

The Spiritual Connection in Marriage

One of the facets of a covenant, which I just mentioned, is a big theological word called *transcendence*. Transcendence simply means that God is in charge—a concept we are approaching from many different angles in this book because it is so critical to living as a kingdom disciple. Covenants are both initiated and ruled by God.

Transcendence is a key principle in the marriage covenant, as well as in laying a healthy foundation for a family. For a covenant to function successfully, carrying with it the benefits, security, and authority, it has to be set up according to God's expectations and regulations.

Until we recognize the covenantal aspect of transcendence in our families—that God instituted marriage and is therefore in charge, meaning that His viewpoint must be our viewpoint—we will never experience the productive, purposeful, and peaceful relationship we were designed to have. We will miss out on the connections made in the spiritual realm.

Marriage is a covenantal agreement created to improve the ability of each partner to carry out on earth what God has designated in heaven as well as for the parties to rule together on God's behalf as one.

Since God is ultimately in charge of the covenant of marriage, the first place to look to gain insight into the makings of a purposeful marriage is God's perspective on marriage.

Most people learn about marriage from an illegitimate source. They learn about marriage from the television, their friends, or the home that they grew up in. If you grew up in a functioning home, then that would be fine. But many did not, so the home—

along with the media and friends—often merge together to form a distorted perspective on the covenant of marriage.

The devil is often behind this distorted perspective that results in the chaos we experience in our marriages, and in our lives. His goal is to destroy the family and the kingdom rule it was designed to have. I know that we fuss and sometimes fight as couples and we think that it is the other person who is the problem. But that's exactly what the devil wants. He wants you to believe that it's the other person who is the problem.

He wants you to believe that because he knows that you will never fix the real problem when the person you are fighting is not the real problem. The problem is a spiritual one brought on by our own sinful natures or by a rebellious and clever enemy of God.

Much of what we fight about as couples has to do with the consequences of our own choices as well as the demonic realm working against us. "One little thing" can easily turn into a conflict that puts a couple on the path to the divorce court. It can do that because it's not the one little thing. It is the breaking of the marriage covenant either through a lack of submission to the transcendent God or a breaking of the covenantal rules of love and respect. If members of a family simply abided by the overarching principles of love and respect, they would not face the myriad of issues that plague homes today. All issues can be traced back to these two rules.

Couples, if we cannot grasp the seriousness of making a spiritual connection in everything that goes on in our marriages, we will continue to rant and rave about the issue at hand. We will continue to focus on the thing that is happening without realizing that we must align ourselves under the fundamentals of a covenant in order to be in a position to receive the blessings that God has promised. Failure to do so hinders our prayers. In contrast, spiritual unity under God brings His blessing.

Family counseling that offers advice on relational strategies is good, and I recommend it when marriages have reached an impasse in communication. But to reverse the effects of negative consequences in your home and lives, and to evoke a blessing in your sphere of family, you will need more than that. You will need to address the spiritual foundation of your family. And this spiritual foundation can only be addressed spiritually by living as fully committed kingdom disciples.

If you want your family to experience God's purpose and blessings, you must function in accordance with the covenant. You must build your home on the foundation of God's Word. The family is a divine institution and as such will flourish when aligned under the kingdom rule of God. The slogan of every kingdom family should be the words of Joshua, "As for me and my house, we will serve the LORD" (Josh. 24:15).

SATAN'S CONTINUED EFFORT
TO DISMANTLE FAMILIES

Seeking to dismantle and destroy the foundations of families is nothing new to Satan. His goal began with the first family of Adam and Eve, but it has since moved to all other families on the planet. In dismantling families, he seeks to thwart the expansion of God's kingdom on earth as well as the replication of God's image in history through His disciples.

Satan's strategy began by coaxing mankind to willingly remove themselves from under God's rule. When Eve ate of the fruit, and Adam willingly ate as well, Satan got them to operate according to their own rule, and under their own authority. Adam and Eve disregarded God's authority, along with His instruction, thus inviting havoc into the home. One small action created lifetimes of pain and consequence. That's how important obedience and submission under the lordship of Jesus Christ really is.

When Satan got Adam and Eve to function outside God's prescribed alignment with Him, the tempter also got them to function out from under God's prescribed alignment for them with each other. Eve became the leader while Adam became the passive responder, not to mention that he then proceeded to blame Eve for what was ultimately a lack of leadership on his part. In fact, Adam is held accountable for allowing his love for his wife to overrule his love and commitment to God (Gen. 3:17).

The result was that both shame and conflict entered into the marriage. Not only that, but nature itself began to feel the effect of sin on the world and disintegrated as a result of the curse of the ground. Ultimately, sibling rivalry in the first family led to murder, which then perpetuated itself in dysfunctional relationships among even more families, causing the entire human race to be destroyed, except for Noah and his family (Gen. 6).

It is only as kingdom men and women function in their divinely ordained roles under God's rule, establishing kingdom families, that will we see kingdom authority operating in the world for the stability of society.

GOD'S DIVINE USE OF THE FAMILY

When the entire world had become corrupted and it was destroyed in the great flood, God chose to start the re-creation of the world's population through the institution of the family. In this case, it wasn't Adam and Eve; rather, it was Noah. Noah's three sons became the basis for the restoration of civilization.

When God wanted to build His own nation and raise up a people who were holy and set apart for Him, He started this through the divine institution of the family. He chose Abraham, along with Abraham's wife, Sarah, as the vessel through which to create an entire nation. In fact, God's intentions for blessing the entire world came through Abraham and the seed of his family.

We read in Genesis 18, "Abraham will surely become a great and powerful nation, and all nations on earth will be blessed through him. For I have chosen him, *so that he will direct his children and his household after him to keep the way of the LORD* by doing what is right and just, so that the LORD will bring about for Abraham what he has promised him" (Gen. 18:18–19 NIV, emphasis added).

Notice that God validated the importance of family to Abraham when He said that His promises to him related to nation-building were directly tied to Abraham's influence on his own children. Abraham's greatness as the father of a nation didn't simply come by virtue of who he was. God instructed Abraham to train his children, along with his entire household, to live their lives under God, essentially as disciples. This is because the saga of a nation is the saga of its families written large.

God so values the family that He would regularly remind His nation that it was built on family when He would speak about His plan in history to them because He would regularly communicate it in terms of family. He would refer to Himself in familial descriptions, such as, "I am the God of Abraham, Isaac, and Jacob."

Likewise, when God expanded His kingdom in the New

Testament through the church, He would regularly do it with family terminology as well such as "household of faith," "brothers," "sisters," etc. The family motif for the advancement of His kingdom appears throughout Scripture.

And when God chose to redeem the entire world through the sacrifice of His own Son on the cross, He placed Jesus into the context of a family on earth—to be raised, learn, and grow in both wisdom and stature before laying down His life as our Savior. Now just as God redeemed the first marriage through the sacrifice of an animal and the covering of their nakedness with the animal skin, through redemption in Jesus Christ families can be restored today when the members who make up the family choose to align themselves under God as His kingdom disciples.

As we maintain the foundation of the family through kingdom husbands and wives raising kingdom families under the lordship of Jesus Christ, we will see the expansion of God's kingdom. We will leave legacies in the lives of our children and grandchildren that last forever.

CHAPTER 11

The Church

D o you enjoy microwave popcorn, particularly while watching a good movie or football game? What always amazes me about popcorn is the complete transformation that occurs of once hard, coarse seeds into soft, warm popcorn. This metamorphosis occurs because the microwave heats the moisture inside every seed until it turns to steam. Once it becomes steam, the pressure becomes so great that the shell can no longer contain the moisture and an explosion occurs. What was once inedible and indigestible is now tasty, edible, and delicious.

The point is that environment is everything. When the microwave performs as it was intended to, the seeds of corn are transformed.

What a microwave is to popcorn, the local church is to the Christian and his or her growth as a kingdom disciple. The local church is the context and environment God has created to transform Christians into what we were created and redeemed to be: fully devoted followers of Jesus Christ. The church also is His authorized vehicle to manifest His kingdom rule and authority in the world (Matt. 16:18–19; Eph. 1:22–23; 3:10). Churches that do not prioritize discipleship have missed their calling, and parachurch organizations that do not plug into the local church are out of alignment since it is the church that is the pillar and support of the truth (1 Tim. 3:14–15).

Since all true believers possess the Holy Spirit, we already have the internal "moisture" necessary for the transformation process to occur. Therefore, if the transformation does not happen, we know that either the seeds are not in the proper environment, positioning themselves for transformation, or the microwave of the church is not functioning properly, producing spiritual heat and growth in order to make a difference. A kingdom church is a group of believers who covenant together to disciple its members in order to model and transfer heaven's values in history. Like a foreign embassy that officially represents the homeland, the church is to serve as God's embassy on earth that represents heaven. Yet the absence of kingdom disciples today is evident by the divide within our churches. In many, commitment to racial identity, class division, and political affiliation takes precedence over commitment to the kingdom.

I believe that the church's failure to produce disciples has led to the rise of contemporary, secularized pop psychology with a Christian veneer. It has also led to a level of syncretism like little we've seen before. Syncretism is the combining of elements of true Christianity with those of false religions, thus diluting and polluting the Christian faith. However, the reality of such a mixed-up and deceiving religion certainly does not exonerate individual believers from their personal responsibility to follow Christ down the road to kingdom discipleship. It does, however, recognize that in addition to personal responsibility, church leaders must understand the role of the church as God's central institution in history for this process to occur. God addresses the church house before He addresses the White House (1 Peter 4:17).

DISCIPLESHIP THROUGH THE CHURCH

Just as microwaves that don't work are of little use to the seeds of corn, so churches that don't disciple their believers fail to leave a kingdom impact on the culture around them. The church is God's officially designated university of discipleship. It has been authorized to prepare His followers to represent Him and His kingdom perspective to the culture.

It is my contention that the road to discipleship is not nearly as complex as we make it. I believe the church that supplies the four vital experiences that God expects each Christian to pursue will assist each believer in becoming an authentic follower of Christ. Those four vital experiences are the church's witness, teaching the Scriptures, fellowship with one another, and worship of God. We will explore each in the next section.

Discipleship is a process of the local church that seeks to bring believers from spiritual infancy to spiritual maturity so that they are then able to repeat that process with someone else. God's goal is for you to become a visible, verbal follower of Christ and then replicate that in someone else's life. The purpose of every local body of believers is to become a kingdom church making kingdom disciples who are having a kingdom impact individually and corporately in the world.

I believe so completely in this goal of the local church that when we founded our church back in 1976, I drafted our mission statement to read: Discipling the Church to Impact the

World. If and when the church is not producing disciples, it has failed—and actually operates in disobedience to the Great Commission's command to make disciples. Similarly, if General Motors is not producing cars, it has failed no matter how good the building or factory looks. This is because what you produce determines your legitimacy.

God's goal is that people be discipled through His church, and the only proof that people are being discipled is that they are changing. If they are not changing and maturing in their spiritual life, that means the discipleship process is not occurring or people are not submitting to it. It is obvious to us when a physical child is growing because he or she is changing. They change in their height, their weight, and in their abilities to care for themselves. Development is taking place as the child grows into an adult. In our spiritual lives, that development is called discipleship.

In our churches today we can get so caught up in programs and structure that we lose sight of the priority of discipleship. Yet all the programs in the world don't matter if they are not having as their result an increase in the area of discipleship. A church can have structure, large buildings, and a multitude of programs, but if the Holy Spirit is not free to lead people in an ongoing process of discipleship, that church itself is actually getting in the way of God's kingdom goals for His body of believers. Such inaction limits the work of the Holy Spirit in transferring kingdom power and authority to God's people, one of the Spirit's chief responsibilities (Acts 1:8). The result is weak, defeated Christians and churches that have little impact on the people around them.

In Acts 2 we meet one of the most dynamic and influential churches of all. This church is vibrant and alive. They own no buildings and have no loudspeakers. They have only the Old Testament, because the New Testament has not been written yet. Of course there are no bookstores or any full-time children's ministries, singles ministries, or couples ministries. Yet this church is on fire.

This is due to the Holy Spirit Himself. Looking back at the dynamic early church we learn a key reason that the church in Acts was so dynamic: it got off to a great start. Jesus had told the disciples in Acts 1:8, "Don't have church until the Holy Spirit shows up" (my paraphrase). They obeyed Him, and the Spirit showed up in great power at Pentecost.

Acts 2 reveals that this church was wildly influential when it came to living out the reality of being Jesus' disciples. It did this through four vital, Spirit-inspired experiences that are necessities for those who would follow Christ in kingdom discipleship. These experiences include the church's witness through its people (outreach), teaching the Word, fellowship, and worship—and not in any particular order. These are meant to operate simultaneously in our lives as we grow and develop.

THE CHURCH DISCIPLES
THROUGH WITNESS AND TESTIMONY

When the Holy Spirit came on Pentecost to give birth to the church in Acts 2, a number of things happened. One thing was that the church, led by Peter, stood up in a dynamic, bold witness for Christ. The most obvious event of the church's witness in Acts 2 was Peter's great Pentecost sermon. This is the same Peter who, just a short time earlier, was too scared to admit he knew Jesus when Jesus was being condemned before the high priest.

Now, suddenly, scared Peter becomes fearless Peter. What is the difference? The Spirit of God. The Holy Spirit has taken control of Peter, and Peter is about to take off and soar in his spiritual life. Now he will become a faithful witness for Jesus Christ along with the other disciples.

If you're going to grow as a kingdom disciple you must ask the Spirit to help you open your mouth and be a witness. You say, "But I'm not bold. I'm inhibited. I'm a private person." Well, the fact is that most of us are only private when we want to be. I've met a lot of "private" people who become very public and vociferous when their favorite team takes the field or the court. In other words, when something exciting enough happens in your life, you will talk about it without a whole lot of prompting.

One reason a lot of us Christians don't tell others about Christ is that we've lost our excitement about Christ. When He is exciting to you, you can't keep Him to yourself. When something dynamic occurs internally, you want to express it externally. If you are a reserved person, if discussing Christ with others is difficult for you, take a look at Acts 4. After the Jewish authorities had ordered the apostles to stop preaching and teaching about Jesus—and they backed the order with threats (vv. 18–21)—the apostles went straight to the church and explained the situation. The church immediately went to prayer, reminding God of His power and the fact that all this was happening in His predetermined plan (vv. 23–28).

Then notice the church's prayer request in verse 29: "And now, Lord, take note of their threats, and grant that Your bond-servants may speak Your word with all confidence." That's a prayer you can pray too. Ask God to give you the boldness not to be intimidated by this Christ-rejecting world, because there are people all around you needing to hear the saving news of Jesus Christ.

If you're going to follow Christ as His disciple, you must be a witness. Whether it is in your actions or your words, you must represent the Lord in all you do. The believers who were in the upper room and who received the Spirit on Pentecost became witnesses. The result of their witness and Peter's sermon on that special day was the addition of three thousand new believers to the body of Christ. Now that's a witness! And please notice that these three thousand people did not come because of an evangelistic program. They came because God's people were overwhelmed by the experience of the presence of His Spirit. They were excited about Jesus.

Their excitement erupted in a great outreach, and many people were saved. Their witness also went beyond their words. "And everyone kept feeling a sense of awe; and many wonders and signs were taking place through the apostles" (Acts 2:43). There was not only a message to be heard, but there was also the power of God to be seen. You and I can, and should, also display the power of God. A true kingdom disciple will have the power of God working in his or her life. Abiding in Christ commands nothing less.

Let me ask you, who is the last person you shared Jesus Christ with? If you can't remember, you need to consider whether you're growing as a disciple the way you should. One mark of a person who wants to follow Christ, one absolute necessity for being His disciple, is to be His witness and testimony in all that you do.

Now witnessing doesn't just mean telling everyone you meet about Jesus (although there is nothing wrong with that, per se). It should always mean allowing others to witness the power of God in your life, the peace of Christ in your heart, and more. They may even ask what it is you have that enables you to live that way, which then opens the door for your witness of His name. But the truth is, when you are on fire about something, you don't need someone to goad you to tell them what it is. You don't need a program or ministry to get you to do anything about it. When a man is excited about a woman, he doesn't need a program to pick up the telephone, or to stay on that telephone when there is nothing left to say. He doesn't need a reminder to text her or show others a picture of her. He does all of this because his love for her is so authentic and deep.

> The church is to be God's fireplace, igniting its members toward kingdom discipleship.

Yet many church members have lost their fire. That's why we need an evangelistic or outreach program in so many churches today. Without that fire, we have to pull, motivate, and inspire people to mention Jesus when they should be mentioning Jesus just because He is Jesus!

The church is to be God's fireplace, igniting its members toward kingdom discipleship. The key question each church must answer is not "How many members do we have?" It's "How many disciples are we producing?" Membership should serve as the introduction to fervent discipleship.

THE CHURCH DISCIPLES
THROUGH STUDY AND GROWTH IN THE WORD

Along with their dynamic witness, the early believers were growing in their knowledge of God's Word. They were continually exposing themselves to the information and application of God's Word. In Acts 2:42 we read, "They were continually devoting themselves to the apostles' teaching." How often were they doing this? This passage says it was "day by day" (v. 46), just as people were being saved day by day. Do you notice the correlation? People were being saved every day. The followers were devoting themselves to the teaching of the Word every day. One impacted the other.

To live as a kingdom disciple, the Word of God must be as necessary and desirable for the spirit as food is for the body. In fact, when it comes to spiritual food, some of us are losing weight rapidly. Some of us are losing weight we can't afford to lose. Some of us have become emaciated. Why? Because we are receiving little or no nourishment.

The Word of God is designed to nourish the believer. The church must emphasize that it is the Scripture that equips us to live the Christian life. Your mind is key to becoming a disciple, because you are what you think (Prov. 23:7). If you have a messed-up mind, you're going to have a messed-up life. The body reflects the thought processes of the mind, and many of us have come into the Christian life with

> *A transformed mind comes through the study and practice of Scripture.*

warped minds, contaminated by an ungodly system. We have minds that need to be renewed (Rom. 12:2). Only then will our lives be transformed.

If you want to fix what you do, you must first fix how you think about what you do. A transformed mind comes through the study and practice of Scripture.

Many of us have habits in our lives that we want to get rid of. But we say, "I can't," because we've been influenced by the enemy to say that. We've been brainwashed by the enemy to believe we will never have victory in that area. But God's Word can change that, if we will feed on it regularly the way we feed our bodies. The believers in Acts 2 devoted themselves to the apostles' teaching, or doctrine. This was firsthand Scripture. The New Testament had not been written yet. So the apostles' doctrine was the authoritative Word of God.

If you are going to become a kingdom disciple, you must have a dynamic experience with the Word of God. God must begin to erase the old tapes in your mind, your old ways of thinking. One way to erase an old tape is to record new material over the old. The data God wants recorded in your heart and mind is His Word. That's why memorizing portions of the Bible is such a powerful teaching tool. Those verses are stored in your memory bank.

You cannot grow beyond what you know. "You will know the truth, and the truth will set you free" (John 8:32 NIV). You must know it for it to set you free. The purpose of discipleship is to gain God's perspective on every matter of life. It doesn't make a difference what the opinion of your church, pastor, or family member is. What makes a difference is the truth. It is the job of the church to give the divine perspective on each aspect of life.

The Holy Spirit is often referred to as the Spirit of truth (John 14:17; 15:26; 16:13). This is because He only operates within the parameters of truth. So if truth is not being communicated by pastors and spiritual leaders throughout our land, then the flow of the Spirit is missing. The reason the church in Jerusalem was so alive with the Spirit was because they were committed to the truth.

What would you say to a doctor who was going to perform surgery on you and he started out by saying, "Well, I think this is the place I ought to cut"? Or what would you say to a pharmacist who got your medicine and told you, "I think this might be the one"? Or what about a pilot who mentioned this "might" be the button to push?

You probably wouldn't use that doctor, go to that pharmacy, or fly on that plane. The reason? Because you are committed to the truth and you want someone in those roles who is also committed to it—and knows it.

Similarly, when it comes to your spiritual life, you don't want guesswork or to be an object of trial and error or exploratory preaching and teaching. You need to place yourself under discipleship and mentors who know and practice the truth. The entire job of the apostles in the time of the church in Acts was teaching God's Word and praying. They devoted their lives to it. These days, far too many of our spiritual leaders spend far too much of their time building buildings, organizing programs, and all manner of things that take them from the study and proclamation of God's Word.

Each of us (not only those tasked with the high calling of teaching God's Word) needs to commit our time and energy to the study of God's Word through the teaching of the Holy Spirit.

The Holy Spirit's job is to reveal understanding and application of God's Word to you. Jesus said the Spirit would remind us of all that He taught (John 14:26). Paul gives us a powerful word about how to overcome the devil and his attempts to destroy our spiritual lives:

> For though we walk in the flesh, we do not war according to the flesh, for the weapons of our warfare are not of the flesh, but divinely powerful for the destruction of fortresses. We are destroying speculations and every lofty thing raised up against the knowledge of God, and we are taking every thought captive to the obedience of Christ. (2 Cor. 10:3–5)

Notice the words and phrases Paul uses here. Satan attempts to raise up speculations and other things "against the knowledge of God." What's the best defense against Satan's attempt to take your thinking processes captive? To "take every thought captive" for Christ. Imprison your thinking within the knowledge of God, which is found only in the Word of God!

This is crucial, because the moment you begin thinking the way the world thinks, like everybody else thinks, at that moment you begin thinking defeated thoughts. Many believers are being defeated because of the way they think. They have allowed Satan and the world, instead of Christ, to capture their thinking. If you are going to become a mature disciple of Jesus Christ, you must make a conscious effort to partake of His Word. You aren't going to get much if any help or encouragement from the culture.

Paul says the goal of taking our thoughts captive is that we might be obedient to Christ (2 Cor. 10:3–6). You need to know God's Word that you might live God's Word. You don't study and learn the Bible so you can pass tests. It is only in applying the Word that it becomes a part of your experience. Just as a student driver can study a driver's handbook all day long and know the theory, he needs more than what's in the handbook; he won't really learn how to drive until he gets into the car with an instructor and takes off.

So, every time you and I open up the Word of God, our prayer should be, "Lord, show me what You want me to do"—not just, "Show me what You want me to know." Every Sunday you come to church, your prayer should be, "Lord, open up Your Word and speak to me so that I will know what decisions to make in my life." Prayer must be intimately connected to Bible study.

If you want to follow Christ, if you want the necessities of discipleship to become real in your life, you need a church to help you develop an insatiable hunger for God's Word. You must cultivate a love for the Word. If you don't have that love, that hunger, right now, don't fake it. Go to the Lord and pray sincerely, "Lord, give me an appetite for Your Word. Make it more precious and valuable to me than the food I eat to keep my body healthy." To acquire a taste for Bible study, you will have to discipline yourself to sit down and read, whether you feel like reading or not. The more time you spend in the Word, the more you will understand. And the more you understand, the more you will want to read.

You know you're becoming a kingdom disciple when day by day you're in the Word. You're not just waiting until Sunday so somebody else can feed you. You know you're maturing when you learn to feed yourself. When the Word of God is precious to you, you're on your way. Church should light the fire; you must fan the flame.

LIFE-CHANGING FELLOWSHIP

The third vital experience in following Christ is being devoted to fellowship (Acts 2:42). The Greek word for fellowship is *koinonia*. It means to "share something in common with others." It means being a part of a common family of sorts. Fellowship is the sharing of our lives with other believers. So biblical fellowship is not just coffee and donuts in Sunday school or a meal in the fellowship hall.

You'll never grow to full maturity in Jesus Christ all alone. There is no such thing as a Lone Ranger Christian, who is a growing, active disciple of Christ. It is not, "My Father in heaven"; we were instructed to pray, "Our Father who art in heaven."

You cannot become a disciple of Jesus Christ independently of others. That's why the church is so important. It is the "fireplace" where one log touches another and the fire is maintained. In fact, the church at Jerusalem did not only share their lives with one another. They shared their possessions too, meeting any needs that arose (Acts 2:44–45). That's part of fellowship too.

True discipleship can happen only by being an active participant in community with other believers (Eph. 4:16; 1 Cor. 12), which is why the author of Hebrews says that we must not forsake the assembling of ourselves together with other believers. In doing so we can stimulate one another toward love and good deeds (see Heb. 10:24–25). An unchurched believer is a disobedient and selfish believer who is limiting their own development and experience of spiritual authority.

If you are becoming stagnant in your spiritual life, you need to be in proximity to others who are on fire so their fire can ignite you. If you are losing your spiritual fire and you're alone, you're going to become ashes. So the question we must ask is, are we connected with other believers who desire to be on fire too? Fellowship is designed to keep the fire burning. There was no such thing as a non-churched Christian in the early church. They were in dynamic fellowship with each other. If and when you are a cul-de-sac Christian (where everything revolves around you) rather than a conduit Christian (where the love of God flows through you to others), you will never fully live as a kingdom disciple.

We need each other because the best of us can get spiritually dull. The best of us sometimes want to throw in the towel. The best of us sometimes fall flat on our faces. "Let him who thinks he stands take heed that he does not fall" (1 Cor. 10:12), because falling is right around the corner.

You and I must be in vital relationship with other saints who can hold us up. But unfortunately, many people have traded relationship for entertainment. See, when you're being entertained, you don't have to do anything. You just sit back and let someone else amuse you.

Relationships are hard. They take work. You have to set aside time to cultivate friendships with other believers.

Relationships are hard. They take work. Entertainment is easy. All you need is a chair and a remote. That's why so many individuals and families are hiding out in front of the television, or on their smartphones or tablets—the great relationship killers.

I think these things are the greatest hindrance to building

dynamic relationships. Whole families never talk to each other because everybody is in a different room watching a different thing. That's what happens within the church family, as well. Fellowship doesn't just happen. You have to plan fellowship, set aside time to cultivate friendships with other believers.

Here's something else about biblical fellowship. Fellowship isn't fellowship if Jesus Christ is not part of the conversation. If you invite me over to watch a football game and all we do is watch the game and eat, we did not have fellowship. Fellowship is always designed to spur one another on spiritually, build each other up in the faith, edify one another. True fellowship always has a spiritual goal: the mutual sharing of the life of Christ.

That doesn't mean there cannot be food involved. Acts 2:46 makes it clear there were a lot of fellowship meals in the early days of the church. We're going to have a great meal of celebration and fellowship in heaven (Rev. 19:9). But the point of it is not simply to get together and eat and call that fellowship. A meal just presents a natural context for fellowship. The question is what happens and what we talk about when we are together. We should leave a time of fellowship feeling strengthened and encouraged in the faith.

True biblical fellowship also includes visible accountability. That is why the church is called a body (1 Cor. 12:1–31; Eph. 4:11–16; Rom. 12:4–6). A body can only function properly when all parts are connected and mutually supporting and serving each other. The absence of accountability to the leaders and other members in the local church means true discipleship is not occurring.

As we have become more affluent and more independent, we've lost our need for one another. Fellowship in the Bible was designed to show us that we need other believers. You can't make it on your own. Neither can I. God designed the church to be a place of fellowship—an environment where people connect with each other. If you come to church just to sit, soak, and sour in your pew, then you are not truly living as a kingdom disciple. When God told Abraham He would bless him, He told Abraham that He would also bless others through him. A blessing is not merely meant to stop at you. Being a kingdom disciple means you are willing to live in connection with others, learning from them and also teaching through example, sharing life on life so that each may be spurred on to good deeds in the Lord and spiritual maturity.

Honoring God through Your Worship

Lastly, but of chief importance, a kingdom disciple worships God. Again in Acts 2:42, the believers devoted themselves to "the breaking of bread [celebrating the Lord's Supper] and to prayer." In verse 46 we read that they were going to the temple every day, and "praising God" continually (v. 47). In the process, selfishness began to fall by the wayside (Acts 2:44–45).

Worship is the furnace of the spiritual life and of a disciple-making church. Worship is basically the recognition of God for who He is and what He has done and what we are trusting Him to do. God is the focus of worship. Therefore, the issue in worship is not necessarily what you get out of it. The most important thing is what God receives from it. Worship does not start with what God does for you today. It starts with what you do for Him.

Praising God, worshiping Him, and celebrating Him for who He is and what He does is the way to get God's attention. God responds to our worship. In fact, God invites us to worship

Him. He has taken the initiative. You will be surprised at the way the Spirit of God will ignite your Christian life when worship becomes not an event, but an experience; not a program, but a way of life. That includes both public and private worship, because both are crucial for growing disciples of Jesus Christ.

No matter what is wrong in your life, there is always a reason to worship, to praise God. Don't get me wrong—praising God doesn't mean denying your problem. If it's there, it's there. But what does Paul say? "Be anxious for nothing, but in everything by prayer and supplication with thanksgiving let your requests be made known to God" (Phil. 4:6). If you want God's power in your life, then worship must be part of your daily operation; celebrating God, exulting in Him for who He is and what He has done.

So what happens when you become a witnessing, learning-the-Word, fellowshiping, and worshiping kind of Christian? If those four experiences are a part of your normal Christian life, I guarantee you will be progressing in your discipleship. Watch out for the believer who is ignoring one or more of those areas.

When a Christian doesn't show up for church on a regular basis, something is misfiring in his or her life. When he or she has no desire to be with other Christians, something is wrong. When that person neglects the Word and remains silent about Jesus Christ week after week, something is wrong. But when we submit to the Spirit of God that He might cultivate these things in us, we are going to see exciting things happen. In the early church believers had the four necessities going strong, and at least two things happened. They had spiritual power, and they saw spiritual results.

"Everyone kept feeling a sense of awe" (Acts 2:43). They

were amazed at the work of God that was going on in their midst. This doesn't mean all of them were miracle workers. The apostles were doing the miracles, but everybody was awed. Everybody had a sense that God was at work in a mighty way.

What were the results? Selfish attitudes decreased (Acts 2:44–45). They became concerned about one another. They began to share with one another. Then people were getting saved every day as a result of this church's dynamic ministry (v. 47).

And let me reiterate that none of this came about because of a program. These were the results, the overflow, of their experience with God. Things were happening so fast there wasn't time to develop programs. I'm not against programs. But programs can never replace the experience of the Spirit.

My burden and vision for each local church is that its people move more toward experiencing God than doing programs for God. The church is like a marriage. You can't just program a marriage and expect to find happiness. You and your spouse can go out every Friday at the same time, but without any dynamic interaction in the marriage you can program yourselves into boredom.

We can structure the church so tightly that even the Spirit of God can't break through and find a slot on the program. The Holy Spirit is the most underutilized power source in history. It is time we release Him through biblical discipleship to do His job of transferring Jesus' authority to His kingdom people. My desire for you is that you will not approach the four necessities of God's discipleship process as just a formula—mix this and that, throw in a pinch of the other, and out comes a mature kingdom disciple.

Instead, I desire that the Spirit of God will enable you to make these things a living reality as you seek to follow Christ and become His disciple through the context of your local church.

Also, don't try to make someone else's experience or spiritual routine yours. God is not trying to make us all act alike. We have a common goal, to be fully committed kingdom disciples, but we don't all get there exactly the same way.

CHAPTER 12

The Community

A s disciples of Christ, believers are to wield kingdom influence and authority as kingdom citizens in our communities. Kingdom citizens are visible, verbal followers as well as
official representatives of Jesus Christ. They are to consistently
apply the principles of heaven to the concerns and needs of the
culture. They are, in fact, kingdom disciples on earth, anticipat-
ing the coming kingdom of Christ on earth.

Jesus points out the role of kingdom disciples clearly during
His Sermon on the Mount when He tells His disciples to be salt
of the earth and light of the world (Matt. 5:13–16). As salt of the
earth, kingdom disciples can use their influence to slow down
the expansion of decay engulfing society due to sin. They are to
do this in the same way salt was used in biblical days as a preser-
vative to keep bacteria from decaying meat. If our communities
are decaying around us, it is because believers are not functioning as the kingdom disciples He has called them to be in order
to benefit the world around them.

As light, kingdom disciples are to be visible, verbal followers of Jesus Christ, dispelling the darkness around us.

Kingdom disciples are not allowed to be secret-agent Christians and spiritual CIA representatives. If accused of being a Christian, there should clearly be enough evidence to convict us because of our influence and impact upon the world.

As duly authorized representatives of the kingdom, equipped by the church, we are to represent the King as we fulfill our assignments with our Lord's presence and power. Remember, He is Lord over all things through the church (Eph. 1:22–23).

This means that we believers are to think of ourselves as kingdom disciples while we are working as teachers, administrators, engineers, janitors, secretaries, lawyers, and coaches. Whatever our career, we are to "proclaim the excellencies of Him who called [us] out of darkness into His marvelous light" (1 Peter 2:9).

KINGDOM DISCIPLES, GOOD WORKS, AND THE COMMUNITY

The primary way Jesus says that we are to influence and impact the communities in which we live is through our good works, both individually and corporately. Good works consist of more than doing good things. You don't have to be a Christian to do good things. The unsaved can build orphanages, houses, give money, and visit the sick. Good works, on the other hand, are divinely authorized activities that benefit others, for which God gets the glory. This means that the spiritual is directly connected with the social.

A doctor who represents Christ, then, is not just a doctor, but rather God's representative in the medical field so those in the medical field see what God looks like when He helps hurting people. It means a lawyer is not just a lawyer. Rather he or she is God's representative in the bar association so those in the bar association see what God looks like when He tries a case. It means a schoolteacher is more than a schoolteacher—she or he is God's representative in the classroom demonstrating what God looks like when He impacts knowledge. In other words, kingdom disciples are cleverly disguised as a myriad of things as they use their gifts, skills, and occupations in their community involvement, political engagement, and social responsibility to improve the lives of people and advance the cause of Christ and His kingdom.

Whether it is praying for and with struggling coworkers, feeding or housing the poor, coaching a Little League team, protesting injustice, or a myriad of other beneficial acts, kingdom disciples help improve the lives of people who are under their influence. They do this not merely by what they say but also by what they do that improves the lives of people in the name of their King and His kingdom.

One of the things we have challenged each of our church members in Dallas to do is to ask God to show them a person who is hurting for whom they may feel compassion, and then to seek to meet that person's need. When they give the help, they are to give the person a card that says "you have just experienced a random

> *Kingdom disciples use their gifts in community involvement and social responsibility to advance the cause of Christ and His kingdom.*

act of kindness; if you need hope, visit our church website," and then we give them our church information.

They offer to pray with the person for any need they express and then look for an opportunity to share the gospel. As thousands of our members do this, the presence and impact of our church is felt in the community in a positive way by His kingdom disciples. It is the primary responsibility for a kingdom church to develop kingdom citizens who make a positive difference in the society through their good works. When this is not done, we experience the rampant spread of evil throughout our land.

For example, hate crimes, as church burnings across our nation are nothing new and reveal the underlying racial temperature of our communities. They began as a way of terrorizing local black congregations by those who did not want them around. They still take place today, along with the addition of an increase in community uprisings, protests, and revolts.

Kingdom Disciples, Compassion, and Racial Injustice

I've been speaking and writing on racial issues for five decades now and it seems that this hotbed of division in our nation, despite significant progress toward unity in a number of ways, continues to burn hotter than ever. Police brutality, injustice, inequitable living, and educational institutions feed this flame. The forms may have changed but the anger and hate (on both sides of this racial coin) remain.

Church burnings were taking place not too far from where I lived in Dallas in the mid-1990s. At that time, one particular community in Greenville, Texas, was being targeted, and a number of churches were burned to the ground. In response, city offi-cials, church leaders, and community volunteers rallied together across racial lines in an effort to unify a community that had divided.

I was invited to come and speak at the town gathering held at the local high school football stadium. More than five thou-sand members of Greenville's population filled the stadium seats. Represented were individuals from both the black and the white communities. As I drove to Greenville that day, knowing the uphill battle this community faced toward reconciliation, I hoped to cast a vision of reunification through a long-range plan centered on the philosophy of the kingdom agenda.

Then-Governor George W. Bush, later to serve as the forty-third US president, had also been asked to deliver a message that afternoon to a town torn by racial strife and hatred. I had not met Governor Bush prior to then, but a kindred spirit was birthed in that football stadium on that day out of a shared de-sire to see communities restored.

This kindred spirit resonated so deeply that in his own words, President Bush said that day influenced national public policy:

I first met Tony fourteen years ago at a rally in Greenville, TX. . . . Tony's words not only helped calm fears in Greenville, they inspired me to begin the faith-based initiative. My first executive order as President established in the White House office was the Faith-Based and Community Initiatives which leveled the playing field for faith-based groups to apply for federal and social service funds. By the time I left office, more than 5,000 faith-based organizations—mostly small grassroots charities—had received federal grants.[1]

I am both humbled and honored to be a part of God using what had been meant for evil, the church burnings in Greenville, and turning it into good for our nation at large through the Faith-Based and Community Initiatives. Since 2001, an increased number of people's lives were positively affected due to this unique partnership of providing social services through the church.

The comprehensive nature of this initiative allowed it to be endorsed across political lines.

Greenville spawned a nationwide approach to meeting social needs through these faith-based initiatives some twenty years ago; however, it was simply the replication of a strategy that had been carried out for years before that. For me, Greenville was just another in a long line of communities faced with racial tension and disunity.

I have frequently been asked to address communities and cities on the issue of disunity over the last three decades—at times in small congregations in local churches and at other times in football stadiums filled with twenty thousand people from the community.

Whatever the size—the plan is scalable and I am convinced that we share a vision across our racial divide. What we lack, however, is the implementation of an organized and cohesive strategy on how to bring about the fulfillment of that vision. When less than 10 percent of the population can affect public policy and the cultural climate as we saw in the legalization of same-sex marriage, it makes me wonder why the church—comprising far greater numbers—is having such little impact.

One of the main reasons we are not is because we do not unite around a common goal or goals. Rarely do we go outside of our own church walls and join collective arms to bring about a lasting impact. Yet that is essential if we want to change our culture and impact our communities as kingdom disciples for the good of others and the glory of God. As disciples of Christ we are to be salt and light through our good works. We are to be kingdom citizens who are to impact and influence our communities (Matt 5:13–16). A kingdom citizen is a visible, verbal follower of Jesus Christ who consistently applies the principles of heaven to the concerns of the culture.

The centerpiece of God's plan for humanity has always been kingdom disciples influencing society. When He told Adam and Eve to be fruitful and multiply (Gen. 1:26–28), God was not merely speaking of replenishing the human race, but to replicate His image through the expansion of the human race in history. This image was to be even replicated on a national scale based on bringing people under the rule of God, and transferring it to other nations (Deut. 4:5–8). So the Great Commission is simply the continuation of this kingdom agenda to the world through the church and the disciples the church reproduces.

Kingdom Impact in the Culture

Now of course, impacting the community involves more than the issue of racial disunity. I use this only as an opening illustration for the subject at large. How God uses you and your church to influence your community as a kingdom disciple could involve racial injustice and much more, including poverty, oppression, homelessness, illness, crime, inadequate education. We are to seek the welfare of the communities in which we are living to improve the conditions of those around us (Jer. 29:7). We are to promote righteousness and justice in society while simultaneously sharing the good news of the gospel of Jesus Christ.

To understand the potential impact of the church and kingdom disciples in a community, let's consider what the Bible says about the cause of social upheaval in the life of a community or nation.

During the reign of King Asa, the nation of Judah found itself in the midst of widespread social chaos. Nation rose up against nation in international conflict. City rose up against city in urban conflict. "There was no peace to him who went out or to him who came in" (2 Chron. 15:5). High crime and safety concerns disturbed everyone. Upon initial reflection, one might think that Satan was behind this turmoil. However, God was shown to be responsible for the chaos in society (v. 6).

The thesis is simple. If God causes the problems in society, only God is the solution. It matters not who is elected into office or what legislation is passed. It does not even matter what new economic initiatives or educational opportunities are put in place. The president and the legislators may have good ideas, but if God is the one orchestrating the chaos—until one has dealt with Him, one has not dealt with the root cause of societal ills.

Much like the culture written about at the time of 2 Chronicles, we are experiencing chaos in our society today. We have international conflict (nation against nation), urban conflict (city against city), and individual conflict (no peace).

Why did God allow such chaos in society? The writer of the Chronicles reveals: "Israel was without the true God" (v. 3). This does not mean there was no religion, worship, Bible reading, or programs at the temple. What it means is that the culture did not recognize the one true God because there were no teaching priests to point them in that direction. Judah had many priests, yet they were not communicating truth about God. The temple had lost its impact. The result was that there was no law, so the people had no true representation of God's rule or governance over mankind. There was no accountability system to enforce or encourage correct and healthy behavior, and so turmoil ensued.

If the visible, physical realm of social chaos and upheaval is to be corrected, the invisible, spiritual realm has to be addressed: God's Word must be proclaimed and applied. Otherwise, the spiritual causes of the chaos will be allowed to take place indefinitely. This is why the solution to the culture's decline was for God's people to return to Him (2 Chron. 7:14; 15:4). The absence of kingdom disciples in the culture inevitably leads to social decay and disintegration (Gen. 18:20–33).

> *For social chaos and upheaval to be corrected, the invisible, spiritual realm has to be addressed.*

Making an impact in our culture is not something that will come easily, though. As Martin Luther King Jr. once said, "Human progress is neither automatic nor inevitable. . . . Every step toward the goal of justice requires sacrifice, suffering, and struggle; the tireless exertions and passionate concern of dedicated individuals."

Since the church alone has been given the keys to the kingdom (Matt. 16:18–19), it is the primary means by which God is extending His kingdom rule in this world through His kingdom disciples. Kingdom-minded local churches must be willing to work together in order to have a comprehensive program that connects both the spiritual and the social. Churches must work together to extend their influence beyond their individual walls in order to impact the broader communities that they serve.

The principle is clear. The more the church brings God's influence into the culture, the more orderly that culture will be. Often we are content to meet in our local churches or local groups for fellowship and study, but real impact will require unity—unity in the body of Christ.

Here are four questions that will help us measure our impact in our nation. Have we, in our nation, gathered as groups to work together toward comprehensive community impact? Have we ever done this collectively and comprehensively with unity from our nation's spiritual leaders? To these first two questions, the answer is no. Have we ever made such an impact in order to carry out God's command of love? Not that I'm aware of.

Finally, have we truly experienced God's hand of national impact on a large scale in the last century? I would also argue we have not. If we are, as His people, to have a collective impact as kingdom disciples, we will need to set aside personal agendas, organizations, denominations, structures, and the like and come together (i.e., without compromising any of the essentials of the faith) as the body of disciples whom Christ died to procure, and work together in the name of our great God and King.

Have you ever noticed how "special interest groups" in our country carry far more weight in influencing our land (policies, opinions, etc.) even though their numbers are but a small fraction of the number of evangelical believers in America? The reason they carry so much weight and influence is because they unite. We may have the numbers in our favor as an overall body of believers, but we have rarely, if ever, truly united.

A CALL FOR ACTION

It is time to set our preferences and egos aside and impact our communities as one body of kingdom disciples. It is also time for more than an evening event or weekend project. It is time for a comprehensive season of impact and influence in our great land.

During the past few years, I have put together and sought to implement a three-point plan for invoking a national kingdom impact by the church. This plan involves:

1. A national and localized solemn assembly among churches
2. Community-based good works done collectively for a greater impact
3. Churches speaking publicly with one unified voice on the significant cultural issues of our day

The problem in our society is that too many people are looking to force God's hand and will into the box of elected officials. They want a kingdom they can schedule, program, and understand, thus putting their hope in the political realm. But God warns us what happens when we put our confidence in kings (1 Sam. 8:9–18). There is no such thing as salvation by government (Judg. 8:22–23).

Even so, the Democrats are looking for a Democratic savior, the Republicans are looking for a Republican savior, and the Independents are looking for an Independent savior. However, God alone sits as the potentate

There is no such thing as salvation by government.

of the universe, saying, as He did through the prophet in Isaiah 43, "I am the only Savior in town."

Therefore, what we need in our nation and our communities today is for His kingdom disciples to make a radical, comprehensive covenantal return to the God of the Bible. We must integrate and influence our culture through all media possible. True community transformation will require the collective cooperation of the masses to leave a lasting impact for good.

One way of getting a jump-start on this collective impact is by identifying the Christian agencies and individuals that already have intellectual affinity and integration within the spheres of typical American society: education, health care, entertainment, news media, literary, government, business, research, family issues, law, national security, economics, community organizations, and social activism. The primary goal of such identification is to take advantage of opportunities of cross-pollinating efforts while also sharing research on cultural trends and indicators. In doing so, we provide a more synergistic approach to shaping the moral framework of our land.

Some of the goals of this partner platform might include:

- Awakening and initiating the desire for national revival, personal responsibility, spiritual integration, and progressive reformation.
- Developing a national strategy of social impact, scalable and implementable across cultural, geographical, and class lines.
- Increasing the efficiency and effectiveness of the mobilization and management of American Christian resources for national kingdom impact.

- Developing a national ongoing prayer movement to support the initiatives.
- Building and promoting collaboration among churches, non-profits, training institutions, and agencies.
- Facilitating research and discussion on national trends within the various media in order to stimulate strategic influence.
- Creating a forum for the sharing of strategies and techniques while providing responsible forecasting.
- Producing artistically excellent, compelling means of storytelling to encourage kingdom thinking and personal responsibility through mainstream distribution channels.
- Leveraging social media to transform thinking toward national renewal and kingdom values.
- Devising a corporate approach to deal with collective felt needs.
- Encouraging thinking about community and national impact as also a local church strategy rather than solely a parachurch strategy.
- Carrying out an annual National Solemn Assembly drawing together spiritual leaders and laity to seek God's face and invoke His hand in our land.

One Collective Community Impact Strategy

One of the ways we can collectively impact our communities is through church-school partnerships. Churches partnering with schools can seek to rebuild communities by comprehensively influencing the lives of youth and their families. This can be done by addressing the education, health, economic, and social needs of hurting people based on spiritual principles. In Dallas we have established such a model.

Churches have one significant advantage in being agents of impact for a community. They are located everywhere. There is an average of three to five churches for every public school in America. Here are three more advantages. Churches (1) are closer to the needs of the people since they are located in the heart of the community; (2) offer the largest volunteer force in the community; and (3) already have buildings to use for community-based programs. By providing a moral frame of reference for making wise choices, churches with their kingdom disciples can equip the community members for social transformation.

One avenue of broadening the churches' impact on their communities is to recognize that churches and schools represent the social, educational, familial, and potentially spiritual nucleus of the community. As people and businesses come and go, churches and schools remain and are ready to accommodate newcomers to their neighborhoods. If these two institutions—churches and their surrounding schools—share common ground as well as longevity, a strategic alliance between the two can precipitate, to a greater degree, positive outcomes for children, youth, and families living in the community.

I remember how this strategy got started organically when I was a young pastor in a predominantly urban community. A nearby high school was experiencing increased difficulties at the time, including delinquencies and low academic achievement. The school principal decided to reach out to me for help. Gang activity had broken out, affecting all areas of performance within the school. After I got the call, I decided to go over to the school with around twenty-five men from our church. The principal stopped all the classes and brought all the male students into the gymnasium, and we shared what it was like to be a real man.

What's more, we did it in the name of God. In fact, I even used the name of Jesus Christ, and the school was fine with it because when things have broken down so much that you can't even conduct classes for your students, you don't get so picky about what you will allow or not allow in an effort to help. After our time together, and after some of the men from the church began hanging out in the hallways—offering help and hope to those in need, plus accountability for those who wanted to cause trouble—the gang activity shut down. Student grades went up, delinquency went down, and the school acknowledged that the church connection was good for producing a more productive learning environment.

In fact, the principal later got promoted. He became the superintendent of the district of eighteen schools, and requested our church's involvement in all eighteen schools. We then organized ourselves and adopted all the schools, expanding our support services to each through mentoring, tutoring, counseling, offering skills training and wraparound family support services. When the word got out to neighboring school districts, the eighteen schools soon became thirty-six, and eventually increased upwards of fifty schools at this time.

In addition, I initiated monthly meetings with the principals and administrators for prayer and spiritual encouragement. Today these meetings occur at the beginning and end of each school year, and periodically during each semester.

One interesting discovery we made in this process was that in helping the students in the schools, we also gained access to the parents. Many of the problems students had in school were an extension of brokenness in the homes. When we adopted the school, we also connected with the families, which in turn allowed us to connect at a deeper level with the entire community.

As our church positioned itself to be the major social service delivery system to the schools, the church provided an avenue to community transformation. We have one of the largest functioning African American pregnancy centers in the land, providing not only prenatal care but also classes for both fathers and mothers. We help people receive an education and acquire job skills through our technology institute, then help them find jobs and get homes. We have a thrift store to help sustain and expand the economic growth in the community, as well as a credit union. We develop businesses and provide medical assistance on a regular basis free of charge to the community.

Why do we do this? Because the church has been uniquely called to impact our society for good. Churches around the country are to set the agenda for effecting positive values and beliefs. One way this can be done is by partnering with public schools across racial, cultural, and class lines and reaching into their community to develop a high quality of life in their area. When churches can set the agenda for the community, positive returns are compounded.

The church and school partnership initiative strengthens communities, and our nation, through seeking to correct improper responses to God's Word, which is the root cause for the dilemmas in society. This successful model has become a national effort through The Urban Alternative's National Church Adopt-a-School Initiative where we seek to train kingdom disciples across the country on how to implement the scalable model in their community. The church and school partnership model exists as a blueprint on how to apply the principles of the king-dom of God while meeting the needs of hurting people through caring interventions underlined with the message of hope.

One of the most exciting aspects of this community out-reach strategy is that it is scalable. The program works whether you have a church of sixty members or six thousand. Our church serves more than fifty public schools because we have enough members to sustain that level of involvement. However, smaller churches can still make a significant impact in their communi-ties by adopting just one public school (elementary, middle, or high school) or by partnering with another church to adopt the same school.

Additionally, the program is cost-effective because the ba-sics of what you need are already in place at both the church and the public school. The actual program cost is contingent on the scope of services your church wants to offer and your capacity to deliver those services.

Whenever I go into a community to speak, I seek to rally the pastors and community leaders around a shared vision for a uni-fied community-wide impact through the adoption of schools. My vision is to have ministerial associations, church denomi-nations, or a group of churches in a local area band together to adopt all of the public schools in their community. I also encour-age them to plan an annual time of celebration where they can get together to share what God has done through the various outreach ministries as well as to strategize for the upcoming year.

The ultimate goal of this vision, however, is not the school but the manifestation of God's glory through the power of His body working together to bring about comprehensive change. (It also gives church mentors a practical outlet through which to use their members' gifts, skills, and occupations to make a kingdom difference for the benefit of their communities. If every community adopted such a strategy, then over time the whole nation would be impacted through this bottom-up approach to community transformation.

This strategy enables us to be the salt and the light in our communities that Christ has called us to be as His kingdom disciples. One interesting fact about light is that it is not as it appears. It is not one color. A prism reveals the true nature of light: when the prism refracts the light, it reveals a spectrum of colors. Likewise, the light we shine for God through good works is not a removal of our color, culture, or uniqueness, but an embracing of ourselves personally as well as each other in such a way so as to create something we could have never created on our own. As we combine strength with strength across racial lines, we form something stronger than what would have been formed alone.

When kingdom disciples operate properly under the kingdom agenda, progress and transformation naturally occur as the spiritual and social aspects of life work in a coordinated way, positively affecting individuals, families, schools, and communities. The benefits derived from church and public school partnerships are innumerable. It will give a visible demonstration of God's kingdom representatives executing kingdom authority from His kingdom institution (the church) through His kingdom disciples.

BECOMING PART OF THE COMMUNITY IMPACT STRATEGY

Dear reader, you can coordinate a church-school partnership training in your area. (The contact information for the National

Church Adopt-A-School Initiative is in Appendix B.) Next, invite area church and community leaders across racial and denominational lines to this training. Then, follow the steps outlined in the training for implementing the strategy in your local community.

For those churches that may not want to adopt this specific ministry model, I encourage you to implement some form of unified good works in your community that benefits the broader society and gives an opportunity to share the gospel.

The philosophy behind kingdom community outreach works. I am living proof. The disconnect ended in my own life and family when my father discovered the life-giving power of faith in Jesus Christ and began operating differently because of it. Our home became different from most of the other homes in my neighborhood because the connection had been made between the spiritual and the social. I am also a product of positive male and female role models from various ethnicities who took the time to mentor and encourage me in such a way so as to propel me further ahead in my life than I may have gone on my own.

This community impact strategy started because I never forgot the transformation that occurred in my own life and family when a spiritual system of belief became the foundation for my decisions. It was then that I saw the link between faith in God and good works for the improvement of my life and the lives of others. In addition, I know the application of this philosophy works because of the thousands of lives that have been transformed through both our local outreach in Dallas and the National Church Adopt-A-School Initiative around the nation.

ONE VOICE

In the Christian church today, however, we come across to our culture as if we are not even speaking the same language when it comes to various issues facing our land. Part of the cause of this is because we have neglected to work across denominational, class, and racial boundaries in order to pursue a synergistic strategy toward cultural impact.

When national times of racial crisis erupt, as they did in Dallas in 2016, in Baltimore and Charleston in 2015, or even Ferguson (Missouri) in 2014, the church should have a greater collective voice in addressing responses to the chaos. Protests take place and anger is often displaced, and yet we need more than a protest—we need a plan. The best way to position ourselves to create and carry out a national plan of restoration involves this three-step strategy—a community-wide solemn assembly, unified community impact, and a shared public voice.

When this is in place, we can speak in unison, calming the anger and hostilities and offering several productive and strategic options for restoration and justice. Several special-interest groups have been successful in influencing culture because they have managed to unify their collective voice among those in government, education, the media, and entertainment. It is time to set our platforms and personal agendas aside when it comes to the matters of national importance so that we can effectively speak into and address the concerns of our day.

IT MATTERS

A story is told about a grandfather and his grandson walking on the beach. The beach was littered with starfish that had been washed up earlier that morning. Thousands of starfish lay help-less in the sand underneath the scorching sun.

While they were walking, the grandfather reached down and picked up a solitary starfish. He looked at it and then gently tossed it back into the water. Taking a step farther, he picked up another one and did the same. The grandson saw the enormous number of starfish littered on the beach and sighed. He questioned his grandfather. "Papa," he said, "you can't pick them all up. Why even try? It doesn't matter anyhow."

The grandfather, hearing the hopelessness in his grandson's voice, reached down to grab another starfish and gently placed it in his grandson's hand.

"Throw it in the water," he said, smiling. "Go ahead, toss it in."

The grandson did.

"You see," the grandfather continued. "You are wrong. It does matter. It matters to that one."

I have reached great-grandfatherhood at this stage in my life. So far I have a bevy of grandchildren and one great-grandchild. I cherish my grandchildren greatly. I want them to know and value their heritage, culture, and future. But beyond that, I also want them—as I want each of us—to understand and embrace our call to service in the body of Christ as His kingdom disciples.

Living full on as a kingdom disciple is essential to God's divine plan of bringing about lasting transformation in a world tainted by sin and its effects. There is power in reflecting and representing Christ in all we do because Christ is the image and replication of God Himself. Through Him, we not only enter into a deeper level of intimacy with God and each other, but we also reflect His glory, something we have been created and called to do (2 Cor. 3:18).

It is true, we may not be able to save everyone.

But it matters, to every *one* who is saved, that we tried.

NOTE

1. President George W. Bush, "Dallas Life Legends of Service," Dallas Awards Banquet, May 2010, video (producer).

Conclusion

Like December 7, 1941, when Japan launched a surprise attack on naval ships and their crews at Pearl Harbor, September 11, 2001, is also a day that lives in infamy in the history of America.

That day nineteen terrorists who had infiltrated our country commandeered aircraft to perpetrate the horrific acts of bringing down the Twin Towers in New York, crashing into the Pentagon, and plunging US citizens to the ground in rural Pennsylvania during a thwarted attack on Washington, D.C. Like the events of Pearl Harbor, those attacks were suicide missions of death and destruction.

On that day the most powerful nation in the world was brought low by a small group of men who in the name of their god and their religious ideology were willing to give their very lives and destroy the lives of others for the sake of their evil, illegitimate mission.

Sadly, those misguided terrorists from halfway around the world, in the name of their faith, would forever change how we function as a nation. As disciples of this counterfeit kingdom agenda (a caliphate), they brought death and destruction, not life and peace. They did so for the wrong reasons, without care for the lives that would perish. Now imagine if followers of Christ, the Redeemer from sin and death, could help save lives in America and abroad. That is what fully committed disciples of Jesus Christ could accomplish as they represent the supernatural presence of the kingdom of God in the midst of the kingdoms of this world.

As kingdom disciples we can bring life, hope, righteousness, and justice in the name of the one true God. As kingdom disciples we have been duly authorized to represent heaven on earth so that this world gets to see God at work in its midst. Our assignment is to advance God's kingdom agenda, which is the visible manifestation of the comprehensive rule of God over every area of life.

This does not mean there will be no problems, pain, or evil operating in the world. It does mean, however, that this world will see what heaven looks like when Christ's kingdom disciples are exercising His kingdom authority as His kingdom representatives.

Movie theatres give their audience previews of coming attractions. These previews include the "hot clips" of the upcoming films. The goal of these previews is to entice viewers to return to see the whole show.

One day a big show is coming to town. God is the producer, the Holy Spirit is the director, Jesus Christ is the superstar, and it will be a worldwide production. In the meantime kingdom disciples are to be like those hot clips of this upcoming show. When we reflect the values of heaven on earth we will motivate those around us to consider becoming a part of the coming worldwide reign of Jesus Christ. And if they ask us where they can buy a ticket, that's when we can tell them they don't have to purchase a ticket. Because of the cross, the price has already been paid. We can share the gospel of peace and life eternal, that His kingdom will receive glory, even as we await Christ's coming return.

Kingdom Discipleship Action Steps

Individual Action Steps	Family Action Steps	Church Action Steps	Community Action Steps
(1). Establish a daily personal routine that includes praying, reading, and studying God's Word.	**(1).** Make having a time of family prayer a regular routine in your household. Use the regular family mealtimes to nurture relationships away from TV and social media.	**(1).** Help members discover and use their spiritual gifts.	**(1).** Unleash the congregation to understand and do acts of kindness in the name of the church for the needy in the community.
(2). Be a good steward of your time by avoiding activities and/or people who have a negative impact on your spiritual growth and development.	**(2).** Challenge each member of your family to make an impact and be a witness in their sphere of influence when they leave the home.	**(2).** Create small groups so people can share and receive love and support. **(3).** Go beyond the walls of your church to take the gospel to the community.	**(2).** Equip and encourage church members to be involved in the issues facing your community.
(3). Build a relationship with someone who has walked with God longer than you so you can be discipled by them.	**(3).** Be an active part of a local church as a family and rehearse together what was being taught.	**(4).** Focus on corporate prayer as a vital weapon for spiritual warfare in the church.	**(3).** Join other churches crossracially and crossculturally in speaking with one voice to justice and righteousness issues in your community.
(4). Build a relationship with someone who you can disciple, which will help your own spiritual development.	**(4).** Take advantage of natural opportunities to instill spiritual principles to family members.	**(5).** Make discipleship a major church priority with a clearly defined measurable and accountable process of spiritual development.	**(4).** Challenge members to be biblically informed and engaged politically.

Individual Action Steps	Family Action Steps	Church Action Steps	Community Action Steps
(5). Set personal boundaries in advance of challenges so you can maintain your spiritual integrity when they come your way.	**(5).** Reach out as a family to serve other families that are less fortunate than you.	**(6).** Have an on-going leadership development program for the purpose of developing disciplers.	**(5).** Have social outreaches that improve the lives of the poor and oppressed.
(6). Invest in tools and resources that will contribute to your knowledge of Scripture and growth as a disciple of Jesus Christ.	**(6).** Develop relationships with other families that share your spiritual values.	**(7).** Orient new members quickly to the importance and priority of discipleship.	**(6).** Adopt a public school and provide mentoring and social services to at-risk students.
(7). Regularly assess your own spiritual progress and make adjustments as the Holy Spirit brings opportunities for growth to your attention and when He reveals sin that needs to be addressed.	**(7).** Expose your family to spiritual leaders, ministries, and activities that will reinforce the principles of discipleship.	**(8).** Have an annual church-wide solemn assembly that includes fasting and prayer.	**(7).** Open church facilities to community groups and events that are consistent with kingdom values.
(8). Share your personal faith with unbelievers as often as you can.	**(8).** View quality Christian entertainment together as a family that can serve as a fun way for learning and growing spiritually.		**(8).** Have different church ministries serve a variety of community projects that will advertise the good works that you are doing.
(9). Be an active part of a Bible-centered church that prioritizes discipleship.			

Note: The Urban Alternative has an abundance of resources designed to assist your growth in each of the kingdom spheres of discipleship. See www.TonyEvans.org

The Urban Alternative

The Urban Alternative (TUA) equips, empowers, and unites Christians to impact *individuals*, *families*, *churches*, and *communities* through a thoroughly kingdom agenda worldview. In teaching truth, we seek to transform lives.

The core cause of the problems we face in our personal lives, homes, churches, and societies is a spiritual one; therefore, the only way to address it is spiritually. We've tried a political, social, economic, and even a religious agenda.

It's time for a *kingdom agenda*.

The kingdom agenda can be defined as the visible manifestation of the comprehensive rule of God over every area of life.

The unifying central theme throughout the Bible is the glory of God and the advancement of His kingdom. The conjoining thread from Genesis to Revelation—from beginning to end—is focused on one thing: God's glory through advancing God's kingdom.

When you do not have that theme, the Bible becomes disconnected stories that are great for inspiration but seem to be unrelated in purpose and direction. The Bible exists to share God's movement in history toward the establishment and expansion of His kingdom, highlighting the connectivity throughout, which is the kingdom. Understanding that increases the relevance of this several-thousand-year-old manuscript to your day-to-day living, because the kingdom is not only then, it is now.

The absence of the kingdom's influence in our personal and family lives, churches, and communities has led to a deterioration in our world of immense proportions:

- People live segmented, compartmentalized lives because they lack God's kingdom worldview.

- Families disintegrate because they exist for their own satisfaction rather than for the kingdom.

- Churches are limited in the scope of their impact because they fail to comprehend that the goal of the church is not the church itself, but the kingdom.

- Communities have nowhere to turn to find real solutions for real people who have real problems because the church has become divided, ingrown, and unable to transform the cultural landscape in any relevant way.

The kingdom agenda offers us a way to see and live life with a solid hope by optimizing the solutions of heaven. When God, and His rule, is no longer the final and authoritative standard under which all else falls, order and hope leave with Him. But the reverse of that is true as well: as long as you have God, you have hope. If God is still in the picture, and as long as His agenda is still on the table, it's not over.

Even if relationships collapse, God will sustain you. Even if finances dwindle, God will keep you. Even if dreams die, God will revive you. As long as God, and His rule, is still the overarching rule in your life, family, church, and community, there is always hope.

Our world needs the King's agenda. Our churches need the King's agenda. Our families need the King's agenda.

In many major cities, there is a loop that drivers can take when they want to get somewhere on the other side of the city, but don't necessarily want to head straight through downtown. This loop will take you close enough to the city so that you can see its towering buildings and skyline, but not close enough to actually experience it.

This is precisely what we, as a culture, have done with God. We have put Him on the "loop" of our personal, family, church, and community lives. He's close enough to be at hand should we need Him in an emergency, but far enough away that He can't be the center of who we are.

We want God on the "loop," not the King of the Bible who comes downtown into the very heart of our ways. Leaving God on the "loop" brings about dire consequences as we have seen in our own lives and with others. But when we make God, and His rule, the centerpiece of all we think, do, or say, it is then that we will experience Him in the way He longs to be experienced by us.

He wants us to be kingdom people with kingdom minds set on fulfilling His kingdom's purposes. He wants us to pray, as

Jesus did, "Not My will, but Yours be done." Because His is the kingdom, the power, and the glory.

There is only one God, and we are not Him. As King and Creator, God calls the shots. It is only when we align ourselves underneath His comprehensive hand that we will access His full power and authority in all spheres of life: personal, familial, church, and community.

As we learn how to govern ourselves under God, we then transform the institutions of family, church, and society from a biblically based kingdom worldview.

Under Him, we touch heaven and change earth.

To achieve our goal, we use a variety of strategies, approaches, and resources for reaching and equipping as many people as possible.

BROADCAST MEDIA

Millions of individuals experience *The Alternative with Dr. Tony Evans* through the daily radio broadcast playing on nearly one thousand radio outlets and in over one hundred countries. The broadcast can also be seen on several television networks, and is viewable online at TonyEvans.org. You can also listen to or view the daily broadcast by downloading the Tony Evans app for free in the App store. Over four million message downloads occur each year.

LEADERSHIP TRAINING

The Tony Evans Training Center (TETC) facilitates educational programming that embodies the ministry philosophy of Dr. Tony Evans as expressed through the kingdom agenda. The training courses form a comprehensive discipleship platform that includes the individual, family, church, and community. Those courses cover:

- Bible and Theology

- Personal Growth

- Family and Relationships

- Church Health and Leadership Development

- Society and Community Impact Strategies

The TETC program includes courses for both local and online students. Furthermore, TETC programming includes coursework for nonstudent attendees. Pastors, Christian leaders, and Christian laity, both local and at a distance, can seek out The Kingdom Agenda Certificate for personal, spiritual, and professional development. Some courses are valued for CEU credit as well as viable in transferring for college credit with our partner school(s).

The Kingdom Agenda Pastors (KAP) provides a viable network for like-minded pastors who embrace the kingdom agenda philosophy. Pastors have the opportunity to go deeper with Dr. Tony Evans as they are given greater biblical knowledge, practical applications, and resources to impact individuals, families, churches, and communities. KAP welcomes senior and associate pastors of all churches. KAP also offers an annual summit held each year in Dallas with intensive seminars, workshops, and resources.

Pastors' Wives Ministry, founded by Dr. Lois Evans, provides *counsel, encouragement,* and *spiritual resources* for pastors' wives as they serve with their husbands in the ministry. A primary focus of the ministry is the KAP Summit, which offers senior pastors' wives a safe place to *reflect, renew,* and *relax* along with training in personal development, spiritual growth, and care for their emotional and physical well-being.

COMMUNITY IMPACT

The National Church Adopt-A-School Initiative (NCAASI) prepares churches across the country to impact communities by using public schools as the primary vehicle for effecting positive social change in urban youth and families. Leaders of churches, school districts, faith-based organizations, and other nonprofit organizations are equipped with the knowledge and tools to *forge partnerships* and build *strong social service delivery systems.* This training is based on the comprehensive church-based community impact strategy conducted by Oak Cliff Bible Fellowship. It addresses such areas as economic development, education, housing, health revitalization, family renewal, and racial reconciliation. We assist churches in tailoring the model to meet specific needs of their communities while simultaneously addressing the spiritual and moral frame of reference. Training events are held annually in the Dallas area at Oak Cliff Bible Fellowship. More information is available at: www. TonyEvans.org.

Athlete's Impact (AI) exists as an outreach both into and through the sports arena. Coaches are often the most influential factor in young people's lives, even ahead of their parents. With the growing rise of fatherlessness in our culture, more young people are looking to their coaches for guidance, character development, practical needs, and hope. For many youth, after coaches on the influencer scale fall athletes. Athletes (whether professional or amateur) influence younger athletes and kids within their spheres of impact. Knowing this, we have made it our aim to equip and train coaches and athletes on how to live out and utilize their God-given roles for the benefit of the kingdom. We aim to do this through our iCoach app and weCoach Football Conference, as well as resources such as *The Playbook: A Life Strategy Guide for Athletes*.

RESOURCE DEVELOPMENT

We are fostering lifelong learning partnerships with the people we serve by providing a variety of published materials. Dr. Evans has published more than one hundred unique titles based on over forty years of preaching, in booklet, book, and Bible study format. The goal is to strengthen individuals in their walk with God and service to others.

For more information, and a complimentary copy of
Dr. Evans's devotional newsletter, call (800) 800-3222 or write
TUA at P.O. Box 4000, Dallas TX 75208, or visit us online.

www.TonyEvans.org

My deep, heartfelt thanks to
Moody Publishers for their excellent
support in producing this work.

ALSO BY TONY EVANS

from MoodyPublishers.com

For anyone who wants to jumpstart their
prayer life and pray according to God's will—
for powerful results.

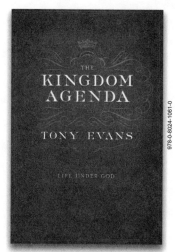

Offers a fresh and powerful vision that will
help you think differently about your life,
your relationships, and your walk with God.

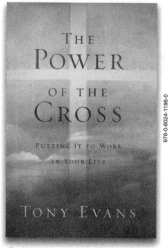

Explains the *person*, *purpose*, and *power* of
the cross, teaching us what was accomplished
on it and what it means for how we live.

also available as eBooks

Go deeper in your biblical studies with Dr. Tony Evans.

˅

MOODY
Radio®

*From the Word **to Life**®*

Moody Radio produces and delivers compelling programs filled with biblical insights and creative expressions of faith that help you take the next step in your relationship with Christ.

You can hear Moody Radio on 36 stations and more than 1,500 radio outlets across the U.S. and Canada. Or listen on your smartphone with the Moody Radio app!

www.moodyradio.org